MODI FOR PM
MODI FOR PM
MODI FOR PM

એક ભારત - શ્રેષ્ઠ ભારત
Modi For PM Fund
એક નોટ - કમળને વોટ

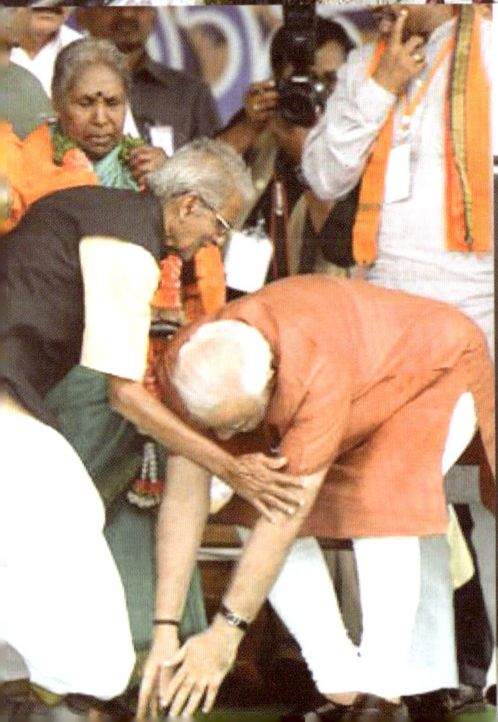

SHARMA

CM to PM
Narendra Modi

Attention Authors

'We Convert Fighters into Writers'. That's the motto of Manas Publications since more than four decades. Our message to the world is that India can win the battle not only by the bullet but also by the pen. There is no dearth of intellectuals in our country, but their knowledge is confined to them only. No sincere effort has been made by any other publisher to channelise their knowledge in national interest. That is why the talent of a large number of intellectuals remains latent. An author transforms his knowledge into a manuscript, and it is our job to spread his/her knowledge by converting it into a beautiful book. For over four decades, Manas has been motivating the intellectuals by publishing their manuscripts and would like to publish your manuscript too. If you or your colleagues have any manuscript ready for publication or are working on it, kindly contact us with detailed synopsis and list of contents. We will transform your work into a valuable publication. If you wish, we can also suggest you the suitable subjects for writing the books related to your area of expertise. Manas is known for its publishing quality and commitments. We take utmost care in production and give wide publicity to the book as well as its author through our national and international distribution network.

CM to PM
Narendra Modi

Vivek Garg
Advocate & RTI Activist

Nirendra Dev
Senior Journalist

Manas Publications
(We Convert Fighters into Writers)
New Delhi - 110 002 (INDIA)

MANAS PUBLICATIONS
(We Convert Fighters into Writers)
(Publishers, Library Suppliers, Importers & Exporters)
4402/5-A, Ansari Road (Opp. HDFC Bank)
Darya Ganj, New Delhi - 110 002 (India)
Phones: Off.: 011-23260783, 23265523, Res.: 011-23842660
E-mail: manaspublications@gmail.com
manaspublications@yahoo.com
Website: www.manaspublications.in

ISBN 978-81-7049-468-3
Rs. 595/-

Designed at
Manas Publications

Printed in India at
HS Offset, Delhi
and published by Mrs Suman Lata for
Manas Publications, 4402/5-A, Ansari Road,
Darya Ganj, New Delhi - 110 002 (INDIA)

Contents

Preface

Telling the story of Narendra Modi and the state of Gujarat is not easy because so many things are fiercely contested. It is not wrong to call him a man ahead of his time. Modi over the last decade was able to brave through the challenges from all corners—political rivals in Congress and other secularists, international community, NGOs, media and numerous forces within his own party.

Initially Modi ran a tea stall with his brother around a bus terminal. Later he worked in the staff canteen of Gujarat State Road Transport Corporation. After receiving RSS training in Nagpur, he became a full-time *Pracharak,* was given charge of the Akhil Bharatiya Vidyarthi Parishad (ABVP) in Gujarat. Here he completed his Master's degree in Political Science from Gujarat University. In 1998, Modi was appointed as National Secretary of BJP. After the defeat of BJP in by-elections, Keshubhai Patel resigned, he took over as Chief Minister of Gujarat in October 2001 and was given responsibility to win December 2002 elections. Since then Modi led BJP to win three consecutive assembly elections.

To describe in one simple sentence why should Narendra

Modi be considered a successful political leader, one must say it's his ability to pluck victory from defeat and rather do it single-handedly. Creditably for him, all these years since 2002 Modi though had good team mates in the likes of Arun Jaitley and Amit Shah, and later supported by BJP president Rajnath Singh; he has been practically a loner in his strive to remain politically relevant to his party, his state Gujarat and also the nation—the 'raison d'etre'—a reason to justify one's existence!

Narendra Damodar Modi has completed around 12 years as Chief Minister of Gujarat. During these 12 years he created 'Gujarat model of development'.

There was an anti-Muslim violence in 2002 throughout Gujarat after reports that a crowd of Muslims had attacked a train carrying Hindu pilgrims and set it on fire near Godhra station, burning alive many.

A statement issued by the state information department says, "In the past 12 years, Gujarat has showcased and implemented the policy of development to all and appeasement to none. Chief Minister Modi has demonstrated how to face challenges and come out of them successfully. He has converted adversities into opportunities."

Rajnath Singh appointed Modi as Chief of BJP's Election Campaign Committee in June 2013 and in September 2013 party's prime minister nominee for 2014 Lok Sabha polls. After that he addressed rallies at Delhi, Mumbai, Bangalore, Jodhpur, Bahraich, Patna, Imphal etc. etc. and highlighted his 'model of development' in all walks of life—education, social upliftment, law and order, employment, agriculture, foreign relations, defence, etc.

In Meerut on 2nd February 2014, Narendra Modi said Congress is destroying the nation and sowing seeds of poison. He promised a riot-free Uttar Pradesh. "Gujarat is free of riots. We have to make Uttar Pradesh riot free. I assure you, we will give you a violence-free Uttar Pradesh," Modi said.

In his Kolkata speech on 5th February 2014 Modi alleged Congress that after the death of Indira Gandhi, Pranab Mukherjee should have been appointed as Prime Minister and not Rajiv Gandhi. Despite a senior most leader, Pranab Mukheree was not even taken into Cabinet by Rajiv Gandhi government. Modi further blamed Congress that in 2004, being a senior most leader, Congress should have declared Pranab Mukherjee as Prime Minister.

In retrospect, from a political loner, today, everyone including the European Union and United Kingdom seem to falling in line.

His admirers say Modi has always challenged the concept of 'status quoist', a feature hailed in Indian polity and instead he had banked on certain 'out-of-box' thinking and actions.

But these are easier said than done. An atmosphere is created, wherein out-of-box thinking and individualistic approach would be strongly resisted. This backdrop of Indian polity only makes Modi's 'rendezvous' with success more exciting.

Now, what makes a politician successful if not great? What has made Modi successful? The real answers need not be very difficult as probably his good synthesis of nationality with development card, his single-minded determination with ingenious use of the IT-tool and social networking sites have all combined together for his success. But it is certainly difficult to analyze and pin point what combination of virtues or traits can make a 'successful' politician like Modi.

Narendra Modi, to two of us from varied background, represents some 'uniqueness' in the Indian political scene in more ways than one. He has a very humble political background and from the hind side, he has or had nothing in his favour. The caste, the political party and even the family background; nothing in normal circumstances would have worked for him.

The party he represents and today leads in the run up to the Lok Sabha elections as the prime ministerial candidate is outrightly dismissed as 'communal' Hindu chauvinist outfit owing allegiance to the RSS in Nagpur. BJP has already served the nation successfully for 6 years under the illustrious Prime Minister Atal Bihari Vajpayee.

Caste wise—he is an OBC—a Teli unlike political dominant castes like Dalits of Mayawati or the Yadavs. On family background, Modi cannot be in competition even against Sushma Swaraj, whose father was a RSS functionary at Ambala in Haryana. Nor does he have the suave approach and sophistication of the likes of Arun Jaitley though Modi is an orator par excellence and can take along the crowd with him.

Thus till October 2001 when Modi was sent to Gujarat to replace his onetime mentor Keshubhai Patel as the chief minister and till the 2002 December elections, Modi was much 'below' in the ladder as against the likes of Sushma Swaraj and the Late Pramod Mahajan.

But those who know him intimately say rather emphatically that Narendra Damodardas Modi always has in him something unique to bank on.

And he attained an incredible success in the last decade forcing the BJP and the RSS to fall in line. And the big debate on what makes Narendra Modi click; one reason that could be attributed is the "Single-Minded Determination to march ahead."

For a politician the confidence to march on comes not from one's family background, the party one leads or even the education. As Narendra Modi himself has said a number of times, that confidence comes from a politician's ability to read the 'pulse' of the people. Yes, he has done that pretty well.

In this book, we have only tried to highlight his vision for overall development of our country and its people because of his past achievements and certainly for the ability to maintain peace and harmony in Gujarat.

Vivek Garg
Nirendra Dev

Introduction

THE COMPULSION TO BE RIGHT IS THE ENEMY OF CREATIVITY, so as the authors of this joint venture to give it a shot to dish out a new book on the broad theme of having the illustrious Narendra Modi as the country's Prime Minister, we opted for certain risks. Will the subject appeal to the readers? Will it appeal to those readers who are regularly subjected to read tonnes of 'anti-Modi' and 'anti-Hindutva' material?

It's altogether a different matter that the same media's broadminded critical observations go for a six when Sonia Gandhi plunges into the well of the Lok Sabha and literally engages herself in confrontation with trouble-making Samajwadi MPs. It is described as a combative gesture of a confident leader.

The same media let it pass when Rahul Gandhi almost compares FDI in retail to the Kargil conflict with Pakistan. The risk is truly palpable.

It's not about politics or the question of political choice between the likes of Sonia Gandhi or Narendra Modi. It is about the relationship between Hindus and other religious minorities—especially the Muslims in this country.

There are truly certain inherent paradoxes to such a situation. In the words of a former Mexican ambassador to India, Octavio Paz, what surprised him most about India was "the diversity created by extreme contrasts: Modernity and antiquity, luxury and poverty, sensuality and asceticism, carelessness and efficiency..." (Courtesy: *In Light of India*). In fact, his list could go on and on. He is also right that the co-existence of Hinduism and Islam is a remarkable aspect of India. But it is also true that the two religious communities over the ages have only grown mutually suspicious to each other. Of course, the political class or the secular brigade gets the credit.

In terms of history, Indian Muslims as a group had a very fond memory of their 'hey days' when enthroned at Delhi, 'they reigned supreme' from the Himalayas down to the South. Muslims have for all practical purposes not been able to give up the obsession of that golden period. "It was an image which spurred them to demand first a special political position in British India and then in the nineteen-forties, independent statehood, should the British leave," wrote P. Hardy in *The Muslims of British India* (published in South Asia by Foundation Books). On the other hand, the Hindus' views about Muslims, even in contemporary setting, are also guided or prejudiced by much of the happenings during this golden era of the Muslims. Even the violence in Gujarat in 2002, according to Hindu chauvinists, and not surprisingly may include your next door neighbours, sought to avenge the 'injustice' meted out to the Hindus during that period.

After all, the Sangh Parivar's much talked about movement *vis-a-vis* the Kashi, Mathura and Ayodhya temples is also aimed at undoing the destruction of Hindu temples by Muslim rulers. In this we broadly agree to a pertinent question raised by Octavio Paz, "Are they two civilizations occupying a single territory, or are they two religions nurtured by a single Civilization?" A very thought-provoking question that ought to be answered.

Now, we are not suggesting in any manner that this book with a certain political plot can answer these questions. But we would like to draw the attention of readers to the observations made by one of the judges of the famous September 30, 2010, Ayodhya dispute. Justice S.U. Khan in his ruling in the famous case had appealed to the Indian Muslims to tell the world about the 'correct position' of Islam.

Justice Khan had rightly said, "Muslims in India enjoy a unique position. They have been rulers here, they have been ruled and now they are the stakeholders in power. They are not a majority but they are also not a negligible minority. In other countries either the Muslims are in huge majority which makes them indifferent to the problems in question or in negligible minority which makes them redundant. Indian Muslims have also inherited a huge legacy of religious learning and knowledge. They are, therefore, in the best position to tell the world the correct position."

Having said these, we also believe that perhaps only Muslims in Gujarat, a state much vilified by the secularists and NGO activists, can truly speak about their state and their Chief Minister Narendra Modi. It is also believed that majority of Muslims in Gujarat are happier than in any other state of India.

Personally Modi has grown a larger than life image in Gujarat and perhaps rekindled the hope among 6 crore Gujaratis that one day their leader can become India's next Prime Minister.

Anil Ambani is actually not the first person to draw a parallel between Mahatma Gandhi and Narendra Modi. From 2002 itself, in the streets of Ahmedabad, the refrain has been while one train compartment incident in South Africa had given Gujarat its Mohandas Karamchand Gandhi, another train compartment incident at Godhra (in 2002) has given the state its Narendra Modi. Probably the people of Gujarat are also torn apart between ideologies and thought process of both these leaders as much the state is today torn apart between its past and future.

Importantly, it has to be understood that the Hindu assertion is also a reality today. The chauvinism has come to stay and it will not be out of context that a large section of Hindus see there is good reason to be assertive if not aggressive. Modi's January 12, 2002 speech at Mumbai's Shivaji Park at BJP's felicitation programme that party cadres and BJP voters should not be apologetic about Hindutva having some relevance. The minorities including Muslims and also a sizeable Christians who do not see this fact are actually not being realistic.

If in every sphere of politics, the general assumption is that the country should embrace realistic and modern polity, it is high time the country's *neta* class also did away with their communal politics. Today, Hindus have many complaints against the existing system in the country. It's worse for the upper castes as caste politics pervades the crucial states in the Hindi cowbelt. Therefore, it is not without good reason that Janata Dal (United) leader and a senior parliamentarian Sharad Yadav says that the Hindutva as a political trump card cannot work in the northern states.

Perhaps it is no longer working in Gujarat or working to a much less degree and only Modi's 'developmental card' is fetching him dividends. Talk to Muslims in 2013 and they say, they have prospered in the last decade since 2002 and want to move ahead.

The message was clear for Congress: Don't expect us to fight your battle against Modi or BJP. The same Congress, who does not shy of raking up the high-pitched controversy about 'saffron-terror', opts for soft-secularism in Gujarat. From 2002 to 2013—it has failed to move an inch away from Shankersinh Vaghela, a former RSS Pracharak, despite the fact that Vaghela has failed the Congress a number of times. On this backdrop, it is important to note that even Muslim organizations have condemned the Home Minister Sushilkumar Shinde's saffron-terror remarks. Shinde's remark was not only illegal but gave India a bad image globally. Shinde like one of his predecessors Shivraj Patil will be remembered for his poor administration and loose talks.

In retrospect, while talking about Hindus and Muslims and their relations, one cannot forget the Partition. The division of India remains a poignant subject in the history of the sub-continent and it will continue to cast its shadow over relations between India and Pakistan and more so between the Hindus and the Muslims. The creation of Pakistan also left manifold ramifications for Muslims for all the time to come and for Hindus a grieving point. It is, therefore, the rhetoric about 'Mia Musharraf' became such a hit for Modi in his 2002 election campaign.

After Partition, all religious communities and groups enjoyed equal rights. But with the democracy, came several inherent problems and occasions when Hindus were at daggers drawn with the Muslims. By 1970s, Indira Gandhi pushed the vote-bank politics to the appeasement of Muslims. By mid-eighties this started taking a new shape and so came in Rajiv Gandhi's mixed signals: Shah Bano case and also opening the doors of Ayodhya temple and then the 'Shilanyas'. By nineties, things had reached a zenith and communal riots became a political terminology for achieving greater milestones.

Muslims forgot quite often that their Hindu neighbours have been friends with them for ages. Similarly, the Hindus forgot the immense contribution of Muslims in nation building and also during the freedom struggle against the British.

But our strong argument that the assertive politics of Hindutva or the hardliners of Vishwa Hindu Parishad or the variety of Narendra Modi are not to be blamed. On the other hand, the so-called secular forces have only spoken about appeasement of minorities—Muslims, Christians and others. The Congress party and the communists are also to be blamed as much as the advocates of radical Hindutva.

Hindus, especially the upper caste by tradition and the middle class by economic status, found only BJP as a political party trying to protect their interest and respect their sentiments. The Ayodhya movement played a great role in cementing this unity among the Hindus to endorse the Hindutva cause. The overwhelming participation of middle class people in the post-Godhra violence in Gujarat only showed that the Hindutva had become the new *mantra* for the Gujaratis and others in Gandhi's state.

Honestly, the polarization was not confined to Gujarat alone. Even from other places, Hindus endorsed the violence against the Muslims. In Mumbai, where the riots of 1992-93 are still debated, many Hindus spoke in private that the English press was constantly toeing an anti-Hindu line and that the Hindus ought to stand up firmly to protect their rights in their own land. It's against this backdrop that we must try to understand the emergence of Narendra Modi as the Hindutva *Hridayasamrat* surpassing one time icon Balasaheb Thackeray. Late Shiv Sena Chief, Thackeray, was easily pushed to play second fiddle perhaps because Modi was also a Chief Minister of a state. The refrain was he is the only Chief Minister in the country who has stood by the Hindus. This is precisely what makes him different from even his party colleague and Madhya Pradesh counterpart Shivraj Singh Chouhan.

Significantly for Modi, his achievements in 'development' and getting the pat from the corporate honchos did not come that easily. In the following chapters in this book, we have dwelt in details on how his detractors in the Congress and the scores of NGO activists said there was hardly any development. Modi has only created a 'smokescreen' about it by making an aura of development.

But the turnout of historical 70 per cent of electorate and the BJP vote share revolving around 49 per cent—in December 2012 polls—was a clear proof that no one was impressed by the campaign against him. Winning 115 seats in 182-member assembly just 2 short of 117 benchmark of 2007, braving the anti-incumbency of last decade and fighting almost single-handedly against all odds and hurdles thrown by apparently disgruntled RSS, VHP, Bajrang Dal and the armies of NGO activists besides the sustained campaign by Congress and a former BJP heavyweight Keshubhai; Modi was able to prove the obvious.

Modi's new found lieutenant Saurabh Patel has a strong argument when he says, the Gujarati voters have not missed the point that the same people who refused him Visa in 2005 today need him and have been trying to inch closer.

We try to analyse the argument that Gujarat is no development-starved state, nor people of Gujarat are work shirkers like in trade union-afflicted West Bengal. But Modi deserves some credit that today no one can ignore Gujarat if they want to do some investment in India. We seek much in depth probe into the question, what makes Modi click—both on political and economic front. Modi's image in the ultimate is pro-development also pro-urban and even to an extent pro-youths—a certain contrast with a 'weak' Manmohan Singh or even mofussil casteist Keshubhai Patel.

Thus, for all practical reasons, pitching Modi against Congress crown prince Rahul Gandhi, elevated as the party

Vice-President, does make lot of sense for BJP.

But as politics is a permanently dynamic affair, things cannot be put into a straight jacket formula for Narendra Modi also. The surprised and dramatic twist and last minute in election of Rajnath Singh as the new BJP chief has added some colour in BJP's intra-party politics. The Modi-Rajnath 'jugalbandi' as was touted in the media has really gone well and also importantly much in favour of Modi. On his part, Modi had taken the first step in complimenting Rajnath on his return as party boss. In his twitter missive within hours of Rajnath Singh's election to the coveted post was announced, Modi wrote: "Rajnath Singh ji served as Agriculture Minister in Atalji's Government. He has always been associated with farmers, BJP will gain from this." At the same time, it is worth mentioning that in 2005, in his previous avatar as BJP President Rajnath had dropped Modi from the party's highest policy-making body, the Central Parliamentary Board. However, at a later stage both the leaders actually had patched up. Subsequently in June 2013 and later on 13 September (2013), keeping in view the aspirations of BJP's foot-soldiers and need of the day, Rajnath Singh had gone much ahead by appointing Modi as Chief of BJP's Election Committee and then the party's nominee for prime ministership. Now the moot question is how they would pursue things in future?

There are other finer issues too. The elevation of Rajnath Singh was actually a compromise worked out by the Sangh Parivar fountainhead RSS after veteran leader L.K. Advani opposed Nitin Gadkari's re-election with all his might. The stalling of Gadkari's re-election was seen in the political and Sangh Parivar lines as a clear case of outright and absolute defeat of RSS and 'partial' victory for Advani.

Gadkari has been rightly described by *The Hindu* in one of its editorials as 'the destiny's blue-eyed boy'.

Now, how would the former Deputy Prime Minister and Hindutva school's original mascot (Advani) play his cards when it comes to his taking a second shot at the prime ministership remains to be seen. Modi has always held Advani in high esteem and importantly in the past Modi has benefited from Advani's strong backing. But with Modi himself now declared party's PM candidate, things have turned interesting if not precarious. However, it ought to be mentioned that Advani himself has on a number of occasions described Modi as a good Prime Minister material. But Modi has an edge as Advani had failed to garner enough numbers for the party and the NDA in 2009.

There's hype in media also about Nitish Kumar factor. But other than Kumar's JD(U), no other NDA constituent Shiv Sena, Akali Dal or possible future partners like AIADMK of Jayalalithaa has any serious problem with Modi.

Even BJP leaders and new MPs are becoming more and more vocal in favour of Modi giving indications that the cadres' demand would only increase further.

Describing Modi as the 'greatest leader' after Atal Bihari Vajpayee to 'manifest' as a strong Hindutva leader, party MP Tarun Vijay said, "He can achieve the impossible through the development *mantra* and is the best suitable PM candidate."

Smriti Irani, another BJP MP also said: "I'll vote for Narendra Modi for PM's post."

Shiv Sena, which otherwise seemed to endorse Modi's Hindutva-hardliner image, said the party would accept the candidature of Modi if BJP cleared it. "Balasaheb would have complimented Modi personally today," party spokesman and MP, Sanjay Raut said the day Modi returned to power in Gandhinagar on December 20, 2012. Another Sena leader Anant Geete strongly dismissed suggestions that projecting Modi could polarize Muslim voters in favour of Congress. "This is only a figment of imagination by Congress," he said.

In fact electing Modi for PM will be a great achievement not only for BJP but it will be boost for the industries and employment. India can get huge foreign investment opportunities as Modi has an art for getting the work done, without hassles.

But having said that, we have analysed how and why the saffron party has to get into the business of fetching more seats in states like Andhra Pradesh, West Bengal, Kerala, Odisha and the entire North-East. These states make as many as 150 Lok Sabha seats and who can dream of becoming Prime Minister without making an impact in these states. In the past, efforts to project Modi outside like in Assam brought in crowds but did not transform these into concrete votes. So here is the challenge.

But talking about the futuristic stance of BJP, one phrase often used by its opponents is: The 'confused ideological warfare'. The other, of course, as admitted quite openly by L.K. Advani, is that the party with a difference has turned out to be party with differences. Thus, the saffron party's biggest challenge is to take a final call on its ideological moorings. It wants to carry NDA along and so some ambiguity remains on whether the hardcore original Hindutva planks—like the Ram temple issue—should be revived or not. The ideological confusion has come down to its stand on economic policies as well. Therefore, the party has opposed the FDI in retail apparently only to be seen opposing the Manmohan Singh government. The differences within the party leadership came to the fore when the Lok Sabha MPs opposed the party's Rajya Sabha wing's decision to back the SC-ST Quota Bill providing reservation in promotion in Government jobs.

How will the saffron party bring things in order? "The months ahead will be as much a test for Rajnath Singh as it will be for the RSS...," *The Hindu* said in its editorial of

January 24, 2013, a day after Rajnath's election as party chief.

Having said these, we try to address more vital question, how much Narendra Modi will be acceptable? More importantly, what about Muslim voters? You all will find it interesting that out of 34 assembly seats in Gujarat where Muslims are at least 15 per cent of the electorate, Modi's BJP could register victory in as many as 21 seats. We have also pointed out more than once that Muslim voters in Gujarat were least concerned about the past, including the gory past of 2002 riots and want to move ahead.

Moreover, the result of Bharuch Assembly seat clearly shows that the saffron party could not have won without Muslims' vote. In this constituency the BJP nominee polled 59.5 per cent votes and unlike Jamalpur-Kadia one could not say BJP won due to split in Muslim votes. Importantly yet again Congress polled 35 per cent votes whereas Muslims made over 38 per cent of the voters. In fact, even Muslims cast their votes in favour of Gujarat's economic development rather than favouring any caste. Except for a few Muslim leaders, a large number of patriotic Muslims have favoured Modi, due to his developmental work.

The BJP won all the six seats—four Assembly and two Lok Sabha seats—where by-polls were held on June 2, 2013. The victory over Limid (Sureshnagar), Dhoraji, Jetpur (both at Rajkot), and Morva Hadaf (Panchmahal) took BJP's strength in Gujarat Assembly to 115 and wresting of Porbandar and Banaskantha Lok Sabha seats from the Congress improved its tally to 117 in the Parliament.

Within a week of his elevation as the head of BJP's Lok Sabha election campaign committee, Narendra Modi planned a tour across the country which started in the first week of July; first visiting the States where assembly elections were due.

Because of BJP's projection of Narendra Modi as the PM candidate, the JD(U) broke its 17-year alliance on June 16,

2013 which left the NDA with just three parties—the BJP, Shiv Sena and Akali Dal. There was a blame game among the allies, a common phenomenon in modern day politics.

All these should make for interesting reading but in the same breadth, we ought to be honest that all the queries might not be answered in this volume.

We know this book is truly ambitious. As we plunged into the project in December 2012 and that too after Gujarat Assembly Election results came in we were well aware of the challenges, and importantly the risk of not being able to satisfy all quarters. So most of the merits of this book as much its limitations derive essentially from both the authors' inhibitions and of course the audacity. However, we have been honest to the core. We told ourselves that knowingly, we would not distort facts to fit them in this book or more so to strengthen our argument.

SOME BASIC FACTS AT A GLANCE

- Narendra Modi was born in an OBC family of grocers in Vadnagar of Gujarat. He visited many places including Ramakrishna Ashram of Belur in West Bengal. He is a great follower of Swami Vivekananda and a great admirer of Sardar Vallabhbhai Patel.
- Gandhinagar has been termed as the Greenest Capital City in whole of Asia. Under his reign as Chief Minister, Surat has become the fastest growing city in the world. Gujarat is now the favourite choice for many business establishments beating many other contemporary states.
- Ten years back Gujarat had a huge loan of almost Rs. 50,000 crore on itself from the World Bank but now it has deposited Rs. 1 lakh crore in the World Bank which proves his credibility as a Chief Minister and how well he is leading the state towards success and overall development.

- Gujarat has bagged the award of the 2nd best state in the world by UN in the year 2010. When every state is fighting their own devils within the society Narendra Modi has gifted a safe land for the women in his state by providing strict law and order to safeguard the women making it the 2nd least crime against women among all other states.
- If at all, this has been the only instance where justice has been served; several high profile individuals across the political spectrum including from the Congress party, Modi's political opponents, have been convicted. It would be worthwhile to note that Gujarat has suffered from major riots in 1969, 1987, 1989, 1990 and 1992—5,000 Muslims were killed in 1969 during Congress regime—yet not a single first information report (FIR) was registered let alone convictions in any of the above. Under the watch of the Modi government, Gujarat has subsequently witnessed a decade of peace, growth and prosperity—the first in its history to be spared the taint of even a curfew.
- The Sachchar Committee has revealed that Gujarat ensures the economic and social well-being of its Muslim populace much better than large parts of India. Muslims in Gujarat have higher per capita incomes (Rs. 875 and Rs. 668 per month in urban and rural areas respectively) than the national average (Rs. 804 and Rs. 553) as also several other states with substantial Muslim population like Uttar Pradesh (Rs. 662 in the urban area) and West Bengal (Rs. 748).
- The percentage of Muslims living below the poverty line decreased from 54 per cent in 1987-88 to 34 per cent in 2004-2005. The two districts with the highest number of Muslims, Bharuch and Kutch, in Gujarat are now among the fastest developing districts in India. In four major cities of Bharuch, 40 per cent businessmen are Muslims

and in Kutch, Muslims own 45 per cent of ship building yard business. Owing to the tourism festivals in Kutch (like Rannotsav), the handicraft artists earned revenue of Rs. 2 crore and 80 per cent of the artists were Muslims.

- The literacy rate among Muslims in Gujarat is 73.5 per cent while the national average is 59.1 per cent. On an average Muslim children between age 7 and 16 years receive secondary schooling for 4.29 years in Gujarat as compared to the national average of 3.26 years and 2.84, 2.60 and 2.07 years for West Bengal, UP and Bihar respectively. The government of Gujarat has employed substantially larger percentage of Muslims (5.4 per cent) than West Bengal (2.1 per cent), Delhi (3.2 per cent) and Maharashtra (4.4 per cent). Gujarat is one of two states where the percentage of Muslims (10.6 per cent) in the police force is higher than in the general population (9.1 per cent).
- The historic third consecutive mandate Modi received reflected the support he enjoys among all sections of the society in Gujarat: 30 per cent Muslims voted for his party which won in several constituencies with large Muslim populations. BJP won 40 of the 66 assembly constituencies where Muslim population varied from 10 per cent to over 60 per cent, and 6 out of 8 Muslim-majority constituencies. BJP's Hindu candidates defeated the Muslim candidates of Congress in constituencies such as Bhuj and Wagra which have substantial Muslim population.
- Subsequently, BJP swept the local body elections in Salaya a constituency with 90 per cent Muslims and 27 seats; it won all 24 of the seats it contested. The membership in BJP's minority wing has multiplied in the last few years.
- A young articulate, thrice elected local body representative, Ms. Asma Khan Pathan, confirms that on a single day, the occasion of Modi's birthday, 7,000 Muslims joined BJP in a single district, Kheda. Several influential Muslim voices

from Gujarat like Zafar Sareshwalla (a leading entrepreneur), Asifa Khan (a Congress spokesperson who switched her allegiance to BJP), Mufti Shabbir Ahmed Siddiqui (Imam of the Jama Masjid in Ahmedabad) have narrated accounts on progress of Muslims in Gujarat.

- V.V. Augustine, a reputed member of the National Minorities Commission, has commended Modi's initiatives that ensured peace and prosperity for minorities in Gujarat.
- Police saved 180 Muslims in Ehsan Jafri episode since there were 250 people inside the house and the mob killed 68—after all missing were declared dead—though they were overwhelmingly outnumbered.
- The media hid from the public for many years that a top accused in this case was none other than Congress leader Meghsingh Chaudhary himself. He was arrested not by Gujarat Police, but by the SC-appointed SIT itself in 2009.
- **Direct Evidence of Congress Instigating Riots in Gujarat:** Congressmen have been declared guilty for rioting and attacking and killing Hindus in Vadodara in March 2002 on 16 October 2003. The accused had stabbed to death Pankaj Chauhan at Resham Wali Gali near Champaner on March 22, 2002. Former Deputy Mayor of Vadodara and Congress leader Nisar Bapu was aquitted, but his son and son-in-law were convicted. Total 4 Muslims were convicted for this—and all of them were members of the Congress. This is direct evidence of the role of Congress in riots in Gujarat on 22 March 2002. This was reported by at least 3 English dailies, including *The Times of India* on 17 October 2003.
- **Role of the Congress party in Godhra massacre:** Thirty-one people were convicted for Godhra Sabarmati Express burning, 2 Congressmen were given life imprisonment and 1 was given death penalty. Abdul Rehman Abdul Majid Dhantia and Farroukh Bhana have got life imprisonment and Haji Bilal has got death penalty.

- CM issued instructions to provide safe escort to the 6,000 Haj Pilgrims returning to the State. All the Haj pilgrims from 400 different towns and villages of Gujarat reached their homes safely under police escort on 20 March 2002.
- **Home Ministry affidavit called Ishrat a terrorist:** An affidavit filed by the Ministry of Home Affairs with the Gujarat High Court on 6 August 2009 called the Ishrat Jahan a terrorist. The affidavit stated that "to fully appreciate the whole matter particularly killing of Ishrat Jahan and Javed Ghulam Mohammad Sheikh it was essential to look at the background and linkages of Javed Ghulam Mohammad Sheikh alias Pranesh Kumar Pillai with Ishrat Jahan."

  Pillai originally belonged to Kerala, was born a Hindu and later converted to Islam and adopted the name Javed Ghulam Sheikh.

  Affidavit mentions, "It is suspected that while working in Dubai he was subverted to the cause of LeT. Javed obtained another passport in the name of Pranesh Kumar from RPO Cochin. Javed alias Pranesh Kumar, though had never lived in Kerala, but suddenly obtained a passport in his previous Hindu name, whereas his earlier passport obtained in the name of Javed was valid till June 2004."

  Javed visited Oman just two months before he allegedly met Lashkar operative Muzammil, is stated in the affidavit.

  Interestingly, the Home Ministry did an about-turn after a month and carefully expunged all references about Ishrat Jahan's alleged links with the Lashkar-e-Toiba in the second affidavit it filed with the Gujarat High Court in September 2009.
- There is no doubt that every party is despondent due to elevation of Narendra Modi—from Kanyakumari to Kashmir. And the only one reason behind this is the '2002 Gujarat Riot'. Did only one riot take place in the country after 1947?

- **Major Riots**

Year	*City*	*Casualty (approx.)*	*Government*
1964	Rourkela and Jamshedpur	2,000	Congress
1967	Hatia Ranchi	183	Jana Kranti Dal
1969	Ahmedabad	512	Congress
1970	Jalgaon	121	Congress
1979	Jamsedpur	100	Janata Party
1980	Moradabad	1,000	Congress
1983	Nellie	1,900	President's Rule
1984	Delhi	2,700	Congress
1984	Bhiwandi	146	Congress
1985	Ahmedabad	300	Congress
1986	Ahmedabad	59	Congress
1987	Meerut	81	Congress
1989	Bhagalpur	1,000	Congress
1990	Hyderabad	365	Congress
1990	Aligarh	100	Janta Dal
1992	Surat	100	Congress with allies
1992	Aligarh	176	President's rule
1992	Kanpur	300	President's Rule
1992	Bhopal	150	President's Rule
1993	Mumbai	800	Congress
2002	Gujarat	1,000	BJP
2011	Bharatpur	10	Congress
2012	Assam	70	Congress

- October 1984 communal riots in Delhi: 2,733 killed, almost 100 per cent casualty were Sikhs, which makes this a Rajiv Gandhi-led genocide on India's minorities; followed by Rajiv Gandhi's infamous words—**when a big tree falls, the earth shakes.**
- Narendra Modi attacked Congress over 1984 anti-Sikh riots took place after the murder of Indira Gandhi. Rahul Gandhi accepted complicity of a few Congressmen in anti-Sikh riots in an interview with Arnab Goswami (Times Now). Sovan Kanungo (IAS) posted in Delhi during

anti-Sikh riots has written in his book *A Bureaucrat Speaks* as follows:

> "...The sight at the camp was unbelievable. Over a dozen hefty women inmates of the camp had pounced upon someone lying on the ground and being kicked and boxed relentlessly; the rest of the camp swearing bitterly. The victim, rescued by the SHO, turned out to be late H.K.L. Bhagat, a Minister in the Union Cabinet...."

- On December 26, 2013, central government had announced the appointment of a Commission of Inquiry (CoI) into the 'snooping' on a woman in Gujarat allegedly at the behest of Modi under Section 3 of the Commissions of Inquiry Act.

  Government failed to name the retired judge for a long time who will head the Judicial Commission. Official sources said a few judges approached by the government to take up the assignment have turned down the offer describing the case as 'highly political'. Home Minister Sushilkumar Shinde has denied that no judge is willing to head the inquiry but admitted 'some problems' in announcing the name. On January 10, Shinde announced that a judge would be announced to head the Judicial Commission shortly. But even after three weeks nothing announced regarding the name of the judge.
- Salman Khan attended the kite festival in Ahmedabad on January 14, 2014 during the promotion of his film 'Jai Ho' and had lauded Modi for good work and also remarked that Narendra Modi should not apologise for Gujarat riots as he has been given a clean chit by the judiciary over communal riots, it means he was not at fault. He referred to Modi as a good man. Salman Khan said, "I have been impressed by the development in Gujarat."

1. Modi CM to PM: A Reality Test?

> "Where does the soul of India live? ...
> No matter the space, the nobility that within is the same."
>
> —Jayakanthan, Jnanpith Award winner and Tamil litterateur

One might wonder why we authored this book on a mercurial politician like Narendra Modi. Well, when we two authors gave ourselves the task of writing a new book on Modi, we asked each other, albeit repeatedly, can we do a suitable comparison between Modi's acceptability in Gujarat and in the rest of India. But it goes without saying that Modi not only has got acceptability across Gujarat, perhaps in the last decade he has proved that he lives in most Gujarati souls—if not in all. And those who do not adore the *Sher* (lion) of Gujarat, he is hated. In short, that proverbial saying, no one can ignore him.

Now moving forward into the future, let us take a look at

this scenario, albeit fictional. But truth can be closer to fiction also, isn't it?

2014: POST LOK SABHA ELECTIONS

The fictional scenario unfolds. Narendra Modi was sworn in a short while ago as the Prime Minister, the second BJP leader after the illustrious Atal Bihari Vajpayee.

Immediately after swearing-in, Modi rushed to the Raj Ghat to pay respect to the Father of the Nation, Mahatma Gandhi. He also drove to the residence of the ailing Vajpayee and according to reports assured the veteran leader that he would need his blessings to discharge *Raj Dharma* (the ethics of governance).

In his first cabinet meeting at his South Block Office, the new Prime Minister reviewed the general state of administration in the country and attended a special briefing on the economic condition of the country. The declining growth rate would be a serious challenge. The new Prime Minister would have to tackle especially given his pre-poll plank of an effective and purposeful governance.

However, as indications are on, he has to carry the coalition NDA along with him not merely for survival of his Government but also to carry out necessary legislative measures on both socio-political and economic fronts. The pressure seems to be mounting on the newly elected regime to cater to basic Hindutva planks also given the fact that Modi's personal core voters since 2002 in Gujarat and across the country has been the pro-Hindutva voters. The original Hindutva planks for Modi's party, BJP have been: Ram Temple in Ayodhya, a uniform civil code and abrogation of the Article 370 for Jammu and Kashmir.

By a quirk of history, the State of Jammu and Kashmir has assumed the status of a pampered state. Well, much of it was due to peculiar circumstances—geo-political situations—and can be understood. But the regime under Manmohan Singh had not only gone soft, it actually tried to give an upper hand to those who clamour for *Azadi.* Without going into much debate, the new Government has to face the challenge of undoing some of these lapses—albeit deliberate ones—by the Congress-led regime only to play their time-tested vote bank politics. Crucially, the appointment of a rather unprecedented panel comprising Dilip Padgaonkar, Radha Kumar and M.M. Ansari, with probably a hidden intent only talks about the Congress machination.

The panel has recommended *perpetuation of Article 370, reverting to the pre-1953 political status and repeal of the Armed Forces Special Power Act (AFSPA).* So we have no real answers to Pakistan even if our brave soldier Hemraj is beheaded.

In the meantime, with regard to the State of Jammu and Kashmir, even the clause of 'secularism' as enshrined in the Constitution and as being spoken every second by secular brigade does not apply.

It's also a different chapter that the per capita central assistance to the state is about 12 times than that of Bihar and as high as 6 times than that of Assam. Even the step taken as a 'constitutional amendment' which limits ministries to 10 per cent of the strength of the state Legislative Assemblies enacted by the erstwhile Vajpayee Government has not been applied to Jammu and Kashmir.

In the recent past, on July 10, 2012, senior BJP leader L.K. Advani had taken a hawkish stance and asserted that repealing Article 370 from the Constitution has been one of BJP's core agenda. "Syama Prasad Mookerjee had launched the famous campaign against *do vidhaan, do pradhan, do nishaan* (two laws, two heads of the state and two flags) for the real integration of Jammu and Kashmir with the country. That we have successfully shed the mechanism of *do pradhan, do nishaan* is an outcome of his martyrdom. We should not let this slip back. And I want that even the Article 370 (that provides for special status to Kashmir) of the Constitution should be repealed," Advani had said while speaking at a conference, 'Remembering Mookerjee: National Call to Save Kashmir', organised by the Syama Prasad Mookerjee Research Foundation in New Delhi. (*The Indian Express*)

Advani had also lambasted the Government and interlocutors' report venting the anguish of millions of countrymen. Today, suddenly we see in the report of the interlocutors that instead of mentioning 'Pak-Occupied Kashmir', they mention 'Pak-Administered Kashmir'. The former Deputy Prime Minister is right when he says the development has definitely 'undermined' the unanimous resolution passed by both Houses of Parliament as well as the Constitution, wherein Article 370 also describes Kashmir as an integral part of India.

The new regime will, therefore, have to take not only closer but also critical look at these.

Now, history is witness that in 1990s, in order to accommodate its regional partners, BJP had decided to keep these three so-called contentious issues in cold storage. So what will be the new Prime Minister's call on these remain to be seen. But a section of BJP strategists have indicated lately that the saffron outfit would like to take a closer look at them now that the party has returned to power. Insiders maintained that BJP's loss of Hindu citadel, Ayodhya seat in 2012 assembly election in UP has made the party strategists rethink on this.

In the pro-Mulayam Singh Yadav-Akhilesh wave in February 2012 election, BJP lost the Ayodhya seat to Samajwadi Party's youthful candidate.

Importantly in the run up to the assembly elections, many voters in Ayodhya when asked to comment on BJP's prospects, had said, *"Kaunsa Bhajpa (BJP), Ram Mandir waley na NDA waley"*. The message was clear, they were not too happy for forgoing the Ram Temple plank just to keep the allies happy.

So, will the temple issue re-emerge in the national consciousness?

Secondly, on issues like Article 370—granting special status to Jammu and Kashmir and the uniform civil code—many say taking a call by the Prime Minister could be easier.

Next in terms of priority for the Prime Minister was to take a stock of country's economy and a closer look at steps that ought to be taken to control inflation especially for prices of food grains, food products and other essential commodities.

In the meeting with senior officials attended among others the Secretaries from the Department of Food and Consumer Affairs and Petroleum, the Prime Minister directed that all necessary steps ought to be taken to give relief to the common people. "Price hike of essential commodities without adequate reasons will not be tolerated," the Prime Minister reportedly told the officials and also expressed desire that possibilities should be explored to review the fuel prices—the increase of which always leave cascading impact on food prices. The decontrol of diesel, poor man's fuel, also figured in the meeting.

A statement from the PMO under the new regime said that the price rise across the board has hit the common man hard in recent months. Mere rhetoric of the political masters instead of solid measures did not help the common people, especially the poor. The Government inaction over the last few years has hit the middle class and more especially the poor along the base of the economic pyramid hard. The new Government will do everything possible to bring relief to the common man.

In the meeting with the new Prime Minister several statistics were churned while a stand taken by some officials at the meeting that the states are not doing enough on their part to check inflation, reportedly, got a snub from the new Prime Minister himself. "So does it mean, centre will wash off its responsibilities?," the Prime Minister asked the officials and pointed out that he himself hails from the background of serving in a state (Gujarat) and well aware that things were at times beyond the control of the states if effective steps were not taken by the centre.

Majority of households' real spending power on non-food articles fell by over 60-65 per cent in the last two years with steep rise in prices of fruits, vegetables and essential commodities like milk, eggs, meat and fish. The food prices of rice and *atta* too have gone up too.

The upward spiralling inflation under the Congress-led UPA regime had not spared anyone, especially the economically weaker sections of the society—the *Aam Admi*. According to an ASSOCHAM survey, about 73 per cent of the respondents had said that their take home earnings currently dropped to mere 30 per cent of their total package and left over amount had to be spent for food, commuting costs, utilities, medical and education bills.

The new Government actually pledged that there should not be any more hunting game—looking for scapegoats as was done during the Manmohan Singh Government to blame on spiralling prices. The oft-repeated excuses: Global factors, increase in purchasing capacity of the village population and that the market could not reconcile to high minimum support price to farmers should be done away with.

All these factors were not new but during the Vajpayee regime, the price rise was kept under control; so same efforts should be made even now, officials have been told.

Among other works, the new Prime Minister would be

looking into various facets of administration, the loopholes in implementation of various policies and programmes and how to deal with the menace of corruption.

The alleged misuse of Central Bureau of Investigation (CBI) during the UPA regime has been the talk of the town and the new Government could soon take necessary steps on those lines. In this context even issues like why there is high price of essential food grains when there's so much of rice and wheat production also came up. Obviously, the faulty public distribution system, related corruption around these and lack of adequate storage facilities ought to be looked into.

The new Prime Minister Modi directed the concerned department to workout modalities to cater to welfare of the neo-middle class and suggested that on this Gujarat model could be referred for a ready reference.

The new Government also sought to take a closer look at the recent upsurge in protest by the civil society groups. Among other such recent agitations in last 2-3 years, the Prime Minister directed that matters concerning institution of a Lokpal at the national level to ensure transparency in Government functioning must be looked into. Similarly, he said there is also need for looking for avenues on how the Government can act quickly on black money front.

The Prime Minister made a special reference to the popular stir in the streets of Delhi and other places on the safety and security of women. Damini or Nirbhaya, as the fictional name was given to the December 16, 2012 gang rape victim, may have passed into eternity but the tragedy has truly raised several questions—most highly disturbing one.

The Prime Minister took note of an observation made in the meeting by one of his senior cabinet colleagues that the protests by educated GenNext often transcend into the periphery of violence and mob culture amid hyped influence of IT tools and social networking sites. It was also told while the younger generation and the neo-middle class had moved forward since 1991—the landmark year when India embraced economic liberalization—means and methods of functioning of the political class still remained colonial. These called for drastic decisions and thus a few critical challenges for the Prime Minister Narendra Modi.

NOW CUT TO REALITY

What happens if these issues are not addressed by Modi in the event he makes it as the Prime Minister? And perhaps more importantly, how does Modi's political detractors and the secular establishment would react to the election results?

Understanding the dynamics and complexities of Gujarat state and politics of Modi has become more important now than ever before especially after 2012 December assembly elections in Gujarat, wherein Narendra Modi romped home picking up 115 seats in 182-member assembly.

Like any complex society, Gujarat poses special problems to write a book on it. There is a social contrast that perceived as a hardliner communal state, how could Gujarat manage a growth rate equalling that of China. The real challenge in writing a book on Gujarat lies in understanding and explaining well this paradox.

Unlike scientific inventions, in social science, there are hardly any drastically new and original ideas. Therefore, this book owes in more ways than one its credit to a plethora of studies, media reports and analysis by political commentators. This book like any social study is based on opinion of individuals and analysis by the politicians also. It also draws many data and references from a latest book penned by Nirendra Dev *Modi to Moditva: An Uncensored Truth* (Manas Publications). But dealing in futuristic scenario, the book deals with lots of ifs and buts.

The story of last decade of Gujarat is in fact the story of Narendra Modi; now we have to examine whether his story—of struggles braving against the onslaught of the secular brigade and a disgruntled party like Congress can really turn out to be the story of Indian polity. Therefore, the book deals with many aspects on expected lines—on the politics of country's foremost headline hunter; and some, of course, would provoke disagreement and intense debate.

There is no claim in this book about any kind of prophecy. Rather it is a collection of sincere analysis. Today, Gujarat is truly a state with immense prosperity and development; what on issues and idealism of secular values or modernisation, tolerance and accommodation—the debate lingers on.

The Sunday Indian (December 16, 2012) described Narendra Modi as "the man of the moment in Indian politics". On the same issue, in an interview with the magazine, Modi is quoted as saying, "... secularism is in the DNA of Indians. We have, for centuries believed in *Vasudhaiva Kutumbakam* (the whole world is our family). Why then the need of dividing countrymen along sectarian lines? The so-called 'secular politics' is nothing but vote bank politics. Such vote bank politics is the bane of our nation."

But is it right to dump Modi as a communal politician and not analyzing the role of others—including the Congress?

It's largely alleged that there has been hardly any attempt from the Government apparatus in Gujarat—especially after 2002—to introduce any coherent moral order. In fact, not only under Modi, the vices like saffronisation of the village home guards and state police was near complete even under Modi's illustrious predecessor Keshubhai Patel and the late Haren Pandya.

The BJP insiders say, the real reason for the cold war that existed between Pandya and Modi was this uncompromising commitment to Hindutva of the two leaders and who will really steal the limelight of the legacy. Moditva is definitely a shining feature of this very legacy one is talking about. Post-Godhra 'handling' had enhanced Modi's image as much it overshadowed the late Haren Pandya, who was also Minister of State for Home under Keshubhai Patel.

And once VHP and other Sangh Parivar elements got the upper hand, the voice of tolerance, accommodation and respect for other religious believers vanished. "The intelligentsia were either threatened or suppressed" and only the likes of Pravin Togadia were at liberty to propagate their viewpoints.

In the run up to the elections 2012, one question was at the lips of every political pandit and even the voters, as experienced by one of us (Nirendra Dev who covered the election campaign in Saurashtra and riot-hit Godhra), was: what makes Narendra Modi click.

Even the well-worn political theory of 'anti-incumbency'—after 11 years of rule—failed to work against him. The foremost reason is of course his assertive approach. By refusing to be defeated he has in a sense emerged a clear winner long before the battle was over.

Look at his confidence. Hours before counting of votes actually happened, Modi presided over a meeting of the outgoing cabinet and chalked out plans for the Vibrant Gujarat Business Summit.

The Gujarati voters were charmed as much by his neo-assertive confidence as by his brand equity 'Moditva'—essentially a fine synthesis of Gujarati pride, Hindutva philosophy and the development trump card.

Even his detractors had to give him credit in the month-long campaign to the polls and even before that Modi, much maligned for the 2002 disturbances, had successfully projected himself as a 'Doer', a tough leader who can command respect, take decision and more importantly, against whom there are no corruption charges. His detractors in Congress and the scores of NGO activists had alleged that there was hardly any effective development and Modi has only created a 'smokescreen' about it. "In the last decade Modi Government has made an aura of development and fooled the people," said GPCC chief Arjun Modhwadia. Another Congress leader Deepak Babaria, AICC Secretary and a close aide of Rahul Gandhi, too spoke on similar lines.

But the turnout of historical 70 per cent electorate in two phases that had a share of around 49 per cent of BJP voters—a clear difference of about 8 per cent over the Congress—only proved that no one was impressed by the campaign against him.

Saurabh Patel, Minister for Energy, Petrochemicals and Mines—a trusted aide of Modi, aptly said: "The Gujarati voters are matured enough, they have not missed the point that the same people who refused him visa, today needs him. Modi has shown that without kneeling down before the Western powers and the Americans, he can make both the US and the UK come down to him."

Picking up as many 115 seats, just 2 short of 117 benchmark of 2007, braving the anti-incumbency factor of last decade and fighting almost single-handedly against all odds and hurdles thrown by apparently disgruntled RSS, VHP, Bajrang Dal and an army of NGOs besides the sustained negative campaign in media by the Congress and a former BJP heavyweight Keshubhai, Modi was able to prove them wrong.

That way, the chief take-away from the mandate of 2012 *vis-a-vis* Modi, most vocal proponent of Hindutva, is: No matter how strong it is and how long it takes, the storm has to blow over one day.

This brings us to the good old maxim that the glass is

half-full or half-empty. This maxim applies to all dynamic human conditions. The beauty of the thing lies in the beholder's eyes. This book suggests that there is a need to come to terms with issues and events. There are both positive and negative aspects to any situation. Analysts often point to one or the other aspect and draw their conclusions. There are those who see even positive aspects in adverse situation and consider them as adequate justification for lauding what happened. Narendra Modi and his admirers in and outside BJP are exactly doing that. At the same time, there are others, who cannot bring themselves to wash off the gory past of 2002.

We belong on neither side. Our stand is crystal clear, if Godhra train inferno on February 27, 2002 that killed 58 *Ram Bhakts* was wrong, the subsequent anti-Muslim riots too were equally unjustified. Two wrongs do not make a right. Therefore, this book tries to underline the need for a balanced approach and move ahead.

To our understanding, Narendra Modi actually wants to move ahead. So do the Muslims of Gujarat.

Addressing supporters at a victory rally on December 20, 2012 in Ahmedabad, Modi chose to be conciliatory but in his irrepressible tone stated that if he had committed any mistakes during his time in office, he apologised to the 'six crore people' of the state.

"If I have committed any mistake during my time in office I apologise to the six crore people of Gujarat. Even by mistake there should be no mistake in the future," he had said. This is the closest the Gujarat Chief Minister could actually come to an expression of sorrow for the 2002 riots.

"Certainly it suggested that he wants to move on, from the violence of a decade ago and perhaps to a larger arena," rightly commented news daily *The Statesman*.

Whether one likes it or not, the 2002 riots have left a

permanent scar on Gujarat. Everybody is busy sharing his or her assessment about Gujarat and more particularly perhaps of the people of Gujarat in the wake of the post-Godhra riots and the two successful assembly elections won by BJP under Modi's leadership.

Gujarat has emerged as an industrial hub and India's top investment destination. We will look into details about how corporate honchos have loved the manner in which Gujarat has progressed under the spell of 'Moditva'. "It is an honour for India that Gujarat Government is the second best State Government in the world as announced by international council of U.N.," wrote N. Kumar in his letter to the magazine *The Sunday Indian.*

He further underlines the message: "Regarding Modi, every great leader has certain weaknesses, which can be ignored because of his contributions. National leaders were responsible for anti-Sikh riots, Babri masjid demolition, emergency, partition and the Kashmir problem. It does not mean that they were individually responsible for these problems."

In 2005, the US denied visa to Modi. But in 2011, that means in six and half years after the incidents, a report drawn up by the US Congressional Research Service (CRS) identified Gujarat under the same Modi as offering perhaps the best example of 'effective governance' and impressive development in India. We are aware that this is not the official US administration assessment but the report had definitely fetched Modi some 'much-needed publicity' braving against perhaps daily bombardment of criticism of his functioning.

In October 2012 in the run up to the assembly elections, Modi truly had got a shot in the arm when the United Kingdom directed the British ambassador to India to visit Gujarat and meet Modi. The Foreign Office Minister Hugo

Swire had asked the British ambassador to meet Modi, 'now tipped as a possible future Prime Minister', according to media reports—to discuss a 'wide range of issues of mutual interests'.

Ending a 10-year boycott over the state's communal riots in 2002, in which three Britons were also killed, Britain chose to restore ties with Gujarat.

The British High Commissioner, James Bevan, travelled to Gujarat and held a 50-minute parley with the Chief Minister.

Interestingly after the poll results came in, Modi was also complimented by Russia. Russian Ambassador Alexander Kadakin had welcomed Modi's victory in the state elections.

Finding itself on the back foot, the Gujarat Congress clarified that the Centre had never encouraged 'diplomatic isolation' of Gujarat Chief Minister after the 2002 riots.

"We did not encourage any diplomatic isolation. We did not encourage sovereign countries to take a particular position on Modi. They did take that position and we know that position. If they take another position, we will know that as well," said External Affairs Minister Salman Khurshid, a known Modi baiter.

In fact, Khurshid has a point; as in 2005, Prime Minister Dr. Manmohan Singh himself issued a statement in Parliament flaying the US's denial of visa to Modi. The Prime Minister had described the denial of visa to Modi as 'uncalled for' and had said: "We respect the sovereign right to grant or refuse visa to any person. We do not believe that it is appropriate to use allegations or anything less than due legal process to make a subjective judgement to question a Constitutional authority in India."

These contradictions of Gujarat being hailed as the industrial locomotive for the country on one hand and also being run down for harbouring an intolerant society with the

Chief Minister at the receiving end of serious allegations thus remain the principal theme of this book. Along with these, what has been deserve to be analysed in details is Modi's not so secret ambition in national politics.

Talking objectively, Modi, titled the *Hindu Hridaysamrat* (the Ruler of Hindu heart) has over the last decade truly weathered enough political storms. Most of these are his own making and the remaining is due to the highly communal frenzy in Gandhi's Gujarat and to a great extent the obsession of a section of media and social workers to find fault with Modi and the Gujarat Government for everything.

There's no denying that Modi is the Chief Minister of a state; wherein the 'Kalinga phenomenon' has not dawn on the Hindus after indiscriminate looting and the killing of the Muslims in 2002.

Unlike Emperor Ashoka, who, moved by the slaughter of humans in Kalinga War, turned to non-violence and spread Buddhism, there was no remorse among the Hindus in Gujarat. And more importantly, that included the non-Gujaratis, too.

While everyone makes a big fuss about Modi being singularly responsible for the hyper communal image of Gujarat, a deeper analysis of the socio-political puzzles reveal something else. If Modi is a pragmatic politician, how can he be faulted? After all, which Chief Minister, can go against the overwhelming near 90 per cent voice of his people? Look at what Manipur Chief Minister, Ibobi Singh, belonging to 'nationalist and secular Congress party' did in disallowing Naga rebel leader Thuingaleng Muivah from visiting his native village in Manipur?

So much has been said about Modi's success in these endeavours that even the one-time Hindutva zealot, Pravin Togadia, was forced into oblivion after a failed war of nerves with Narendra Modi. Gujarat watchers see much bigger games behind all these. While Modi and BJP has been in power for more than a decade in Gujarat, a key frontal organisation of the Sangh, the VHP has been rendered rather playing second fiddle, if not totally out of discord.

The Chief Minister has not only sidelined Togadia, who had taken a very aggressive stance against Advani's 'Jinnah secular' remarks; but in the 2012 assembly elections, VHP's foot-soldiers were virtually divided with bulk of them pledging support to Modi *vis-a-vis* Keshubhai Patel-floated Gujarat Parivartan Party (GPP). It goes without saying, prior to the Modi phenomenon in Gujarat, the VHP used to call the shots in politics as well as in the running of various wings of Government including the Home Guards and perhaps also the Police.

Even post-Godhra bandh on February 28, 2002 was called by VHP and BJP had only faithfully toed the Sangh organisational line. And what followed, the rest is history. The VHP supported Modi wholeheartedly during the 2002 assembly elections, Modi's Gaurav Yatra prior to the polls that year had the backing of VHP foot-soldiers. But since then Modi has chosen to ignore and sideline the VHP and its leaders, especially the one-time vocal Pravin Togadia.

In 2005, Gordhan Zadafia, a one-time Modi confidant, had refused to take oath as minister ostensibly at the instance of Togadia and former BJP stalwart Keshubhai Patel. It's in this backdrop that the former BJP strategist Govindacharya campaigned against Modi.

The state's main opposition Congress also has been trying to play to the audience without offering itself as a viable 'secular' alternative. While Sonia Gandhi's party goes overboard in appeasing the Muslims by blaming the Sangh Parivar for Malegaon and Hyderabad blasts, it turned to an ex-RSS man Shankersinh Vaghela to take on Modi, even in 2012. Later on we will discuss Vaghela's politics of opportunism too.

Curiously, the Congress party's best known RSS-baiter Digvijaya Singh maintained a studied silence on it. However, we have an instance, wherein Mani Shankar Aiyar, a known Sonia-confidant, has spoken against Congress going with 'soft secularism' in Gujarat.

At times, during 2012 polls, the Congress party played a rather confused game. It maintained a low-profile campaign mostly avoiding taking on Modi on the communalism-secularism platform. Interestingly it also sided with GPP—another pro-RSS outfit of Keshubhai Patel.

Fresh from Gujarat election coverage, Nirendra Dev reported for his paper *The Statesman* on December 6, 2012 a story under the headline, 'Rivals Come Together to Fight Modi'.

In this story, it was pointed out correctly that politicians and political parties are often strange bedfellows. In the case of the Congress-Gujarat Parivartan Party (GPP) alliance—from overt or covert—it's truly a case of sleeping with the enemy.

The GPP led by former BJP satrap Keshubhai Patel represents the antithesis of Congress ideology and philosophy. The GPP is not only a caste-based outfit floated by a former Hindutva champion, it swears by the ideologies of Sangh Parivar ideologue Deen Dayal Upadhyaya.

GPP leader Gordhan Zadafia, number two in his party after Keshubhai, in fact charges the Narendra Modi regime with 'compromising' on the principles of Hindutva in order to project himself as a future Prime Ministerial candidate.

"Our party, the GPP, is a more genuine Hindutva party, Narendra Modi has reduced the BJP in Gujarat to a party of the Ambanis and Adanis. Where is Hindutva?" asked Chetan Trivedi, campaign in-charge of the GPP in rural Bhavnagar.

The question is a puzzle for Congress leaders too. "I know what you are asking," said Ilyas Qureshi, spokesman for the Ahmedabad unit of Congress, adding, "but in electoral politics, an enemy's enemy is a friend. You should not read anything more."

Privately, Congress leaders admitted that a 'greater catastrophe' will occur if the GPP and the Congress have to form an alternative. "That Plan B has not been worked out yet," said some leaders adding, "it will be difficult to stomach a Keshubhai-led Government with the Congress supporting it." (*The Statesman*, December 7, 2012)

On the other hand, the Congress party sought to bank on the Governor's office in Gandhinagar and resorted to backroom strategy and the use of Lokayukta to fight Modi.

The Lokayukta controversy can be seen in that perspective wherein Congress had sought to make suitable and selective use, if not misuse, of the office of Governor to its benefit and to embarrass the Modi regime. Is the Modi camp entirely wrong when it says that Congress is trying to get rid of Modi from the throne of Gandhinagar through backdoor—the use of Lokayukta office?

Now this element of polarisation has gone beyond a point. No longer it is merely on religious plane. These days in Gujarat, it is well-perceived thought that there are two sets of people—one who approve of Narendra Modi and the other, albeit in minority, who do not. The three-day *Sadbhavna* Fast by the Gujarat Chief Minister from September 17, 2011 brought that to clear focus, with an explicit message that Modi is eyeing beyond Gujarat.

By trying to focus on the 'Gujarat's development model' for a prosperous India, he had made his intentions clear. Many suggest, unlike the past—armed with the latest victory—the Gujarat Chief Minister has perhaps been able to sideline his detractors in the party. In a way, he is already much ahead of others in the race and also against his one-time mentor and a great benefactor L.K. Advani.

On December 18, 2012, two days before the election results came in, *Ucan News* reported: "Stain of anti-Muslim violence unlikely to be an obstacle to Narendra Modi's ambitions."

It further said, "The result will decide whether Modi ... will serve a third straight term as the state Chief Minister. It could also determine his future at national level."

Writing in *The Indian Express,* analyst Pratap Bhanu Mehta said Modi's "triumph is an emphatic political achievement."

"He, like a handful of other Chief Ministers brilliantly grasped the fact that Indian politics is deeply aspirational. It rewards governance."

The Hindustan Times reported—"The win proved that Mr. Modi cannot be described as just another regional leader anymore."

Acclaimed international magazine *Time* under a catchy headline 'Is Narendra Modi a Step Closer to Being India's Next Prime Minister?' wrote: "Few figures in Indian politics have the kind of devoted following that Modi, 62, enjoys today. The feverishly loyal supporters who gave their Chief Minister another run in office this week believe he has turned the state around, creating a rare, business-friendly environment that has brought money, infrastructure and much needed jobs to this important coastal state."

The magazine did not miss the point that in his victory rally address, Modi thundered: "Development won today". "There was a thinking in our politics that good economics is bad politics," Modi also said.

On December 27, 2012, Modi landed in Delhi for the National Development Council meeting addressed among others by the Prime Minister Dr. Manmohan Singh. For obvious reasons, Modi stole much of the limelight—at least in the media; barring the walkout from the NDC meet by Tamil Nadu Chief Minister and AIADMK supremo Jayalalithaa.

On its part, BJP sought to set the stage for a definite and bigger role for their new found mascot, Narendra Modi with the party workers chanting "PM! PM!" slogans repeatedly at the party Headquarters on Ashoka Road, where the Gujarat Chief Minister once served as party's backroom strategist and General Secretary.

While addressing the gathering, Modi thanked the party's organisational strength for its support bringing such a sea-change in the life and career of an 'ordinary worker' like him, the party President Nitin Gadkari, who for sometime shared a 'blow hot, blow cold' relationship with the Chief Minister, thanked the latter for the *tohfa* (gift) he had got in the form of an emphatic victory for a third time.

"I am one of you...," Modi said in his brief speech pointing out how the sheer hard work and good governance in Gujarat has emerged as a model for the rest of the country today.

Inviting BJP foot-soldiers from Delhi to visit Gujarat to get a first hand account of his administration, the Chief Minister took a potshot at the Manmohan Singh Government alleging a 'disappointing' mood is prevailing in the country today.

"Desh me nirasha ka mahol hae ... yeh sarkar raste aisa khod rahe hain ... jo desh ko gaddhe mein le jaegaa" (there is a mood of despondency, this Government is doing everything to take the country backward), he had said.

While he had pledged to scale new heights for his state, the party's new supposed 'vote-catcher' after illustrious Atal Bihari Vajpayee, said, "If China can become a manufacturing hub; Gujarat too can."

He urged his party workers to 'emulate Gujarat model', a statement readily endorsed by party chief Gadkari, who patted Modi saying, "Gujarat is an example before the nation today."

The felicitation for Modi at the party headquarter is unprecedented and a veiled indication of party's intent especially due to the overwhelming demand of party's foot-soldiers to elevate him as the Prime Ministerial candidate.

Earlier at Vigyan Bhawan, the venue of NDC meet, Modi skirted a direct question on speculation of him contesting the next Lok Sabha election from Lucknow. 'Dhanyavad'—was his mere response, but significantly, he did not rule it out outright. The sitting Lucknow MP, Lalji Tandon, onetime Vajpayee associate, had said only days before that he would be too happy if Modi contests from Lucknow.

In his speech at the NDC meet, Modi hit out at the Centre's policies for 'lacking urgency or seriousness' in tackling economic crises. Stating that a 'sense of pessimism' ruled in the 12th Plan, he said, "It seems that there is no urgency or seriousness in tackling economic crises. There has been a virtual lack of direction in the macroeconomic management of the country."

He slammed the centre for giving up the initial target of 9 per cent GDP growth and said "it was not impossible to achieve if we had the political will to do what is necessary."

At the party Headquarters also, he raked up the same issue and mocked at the centre saying, "the present growth rate is 7.9 per cent. Now they want to raise it to 8.2 per cent. So to ensure this meagre jump of 0.3 per cent, today they called all the Chief Ministers from all over the country," he had said in his inimitable style amid party workers screaming 'shame-shame'.

He said under UPA regime there is a 'mismatch' between Government's vision and country's need and added while 65 per cent of population were youth force, 'the Government had neither dream nor the political will' to galvanize the youth force.

During his stay in the capital, the Gujarat Chief Minister

also met senior party leaders L.K. Advani, Sushma Swaraj and Murli Manohar Joshi.

In fact, Modi has made his 'political will' *vis-a-vis* development and governance a catch point to scale newer heights in political graph. It is this elementary matter that would work as a 'catalyst of change' for him.

Today, as they say, Gujarat is the only state in India where both big businesses and small farmers can rely on uninterrupted power supply for nearly 24 hours a day. In 10 years, Gujarat's auto industry has grown from one modest plant to an expected capacity of 7,00,000 cars in 2014, including billion-dollar investments announced last year by Ford and Peugeot.

2. Narendra Modi: The Headline Hunter

In 2013-14, Narendra Modi exemplifies the saying that not every noun needs adjectives. But he has a stock full of those. 'Gujarat ka Sher' (lion of Gujarat), 'Gujarat ka Gaurav' (pride of Gujarat), 'Chhota Sardar' (clean Chief Minister) and a 'CEO' are all on the positive realm. Well, there are a few on the negativity too. But it goes without stating that Modi's rise is an example of an old adage that human life is full of miracles. One really will never know what miracle and pleasant surprises are stored in some people's life. But all that do come with hard work and importantly by playing the cards well.

Thanks to the post-Godhra riots and subsequent polarisation, politics of Gujarat turned overwhelmingly in favour of Modi. He not only helped BJP score a hat-trick to take control of the western border state in 2002 December polls, but the party vote share reached a peak at 51 per cent followed by 44.8 per cent in 1998, 42.5 per cent in 1995 and 26.7 per cent in 1990.

In 2007 polls, BJP vote share was 49.1 per cent winning 117 seats and in 2012 it was 48 per cent with 116 seats. Gujarat is today better known as a Hindu laboratory but according to Modi's admirers also as a 'development model'. We have seen earlier, how BJP chief Nitin Gadkari says that Gujarat has emerged as an example for the rest of the country in terms of development.

Personally Modi has grown a larger than life image since August 2001, when he was first appointed as the Chief Minister, the party had faced a rather indifferent electorate among the same Gujaratis. In 2002, it was a neo-assertive Modi, who riding on the wave of 'Hindu consolidation' recorded a resounding victory even in Northern region and tribal belts of Panchmahal and Dahod showing post-Godhra riots had sought to bring even tribals and OBCs under the influence of Hindutva school of thought. BJP won Godhra, from where it all started, with Bajrang Dal stalwart Haresh Bhatt openly declaring that it was 'Hindutva' which bagged him the seat.

Prior to that, before he was made the Chief Minister by an embattled BJP leadership replacing Gujarat old-hand Keshubhai Patel, the party had made him a general secretary. Thus, it was only after the 2002 riots and the December 2002 elections that year—with much ease the vacant third slot in BJP hierarchy after Vajpayee and his deputy Advani, went to Modi, may be. And there was no great competition unlike post-2004, after BJP lost the crucial Lok Sabha poll. Kalyan Singh, hero of Ram Temple agitation, had already burnt his fingers by making personal attacks against Vajpayee and another RSS-favoured and the then Human Resource Development Minister Murli Manohar Joshi was also sidelined.

The results of Assembly elections of December 2002 also marked a beginning of talks about Gujarat formula elsewhere in the country. This simply also meant making Modi, the party's new vote catcher. None other than the then Prime Minister Vajpayee himself gave credence to these theories when in his characteristic mixed signals speech, he had said, "People wanted BJP and certainly not the negativism of Congress", and also had posed a question whether 'Gujarat model' should be repeated elsewhere. Not surprisingly, it was the same Vajpayee, who on 5 April 2002, at Shah Alam relief camp speech in Ahmedabad, had lamented at the anti-Muslim riots and wondered with 'what face' he could go abroad.

Looking back, the political growth of the man has truly come as unpredictable as has been his metamorphosis into an accomplished *neta* from a humble 'chai wallah' (tea vendor) from little known Mehsana—where Modi had turned RSS Pracharak (roughly translated into a propagator) at the age of 22.

"I am an organisation man," he had said umpteen times in the last decade well-aware that like life, political career, is also full of miracles wherein much surprises—including pleasant and unpleasant ones—are often stored in. "Necessity is the biggest driver in life and also a giver," he had remarked casually in 2002, a day after Akshardham temple was attacked in Gandhinagar. He could be banking on these 'surprise' factors of destiny; but a man of action that he is—Modi has kept himself eyeing for the national leadership without any hesitation or any ambiguity.

Till date, he has not ruled out such a possibility. He only says, "I have not yet thought of these. My mission in life is to give my best to the country; and I am trying that to the best of my ability," he had said in an interview.

There are already talks about his chances of contesting

Lok Sabha election from Lucknow, something Modi has not bothered to deny. There are also talks about his plans to designate either Anandiben Patel or Saurav Patel as his successor in Gujarat—once he makes a nationwide plunge.

Modi's ability to judge people's pulse; something he himself takes pride in rather openly, is exemplary.

Given that context, many feel he has plunged into national politics only when he is 'sure' of a certain victory and walking into the 7 Race Course Road, the official residence of the Prime Minister.

During 2002 days, when he was once questioned about his *Hum panch hamare pachis* remark attributed to Muslims largely; his reply was cryptic: "I know people's pulse ... I have never said Muslims. It was a comment on family planning and people of Gujarat liked and endorsed what I said." True to somewhat like Vajpayee characteristic, Modi was only telling half-truth and that too very cleverly.

It's true, the people of Gujarat really endorsed his comments against unstructured family life of the Muslims, but Modi was concealing the obvious fact that the target of his tirade was the battered minority community only.

Similarly, in the run up to the 2012 polls, he dubbed Congress President Sonia Gandhi's trusted aide Ahmed Patel as 'Ahmed Mia Patel', and if the people's mandate is an indication, the voters did not mind such statements.

Similarly his Mia Musharraf rhetoric is considered popular in terms of electoral backing.

HINDU HRIDAYASAMRAT

The large scale criticism and virtual antagonism of a section of media and the Western world towards him has not deterred his commitment to the Hindutva. In a public meeting at Shivaji Park in Mumbai on 12 January 2003, he was emphatic on this score and urged the people not to be apologetic about 'Hindutva'.

Thus, it is not wrong to say that the 'making of brand Moditva' owes its origin to the polarized polity of 2002 in Gujarat.

Till 27 February 2002, Narendra Modi was another BJP leader and a Chief Minister. But his moment came when the Ahmedabad-bound Sabarmati Express from Faizabad was attacked by Muslims at Godhra station killing 58 *Kar Sevaks,* later to be described as *Ram Bhakts.*

He visited Godhra station and said his government viewed the attack on *Ram Bhakts* seriously, who were returning from Ayodhya. His government termed the incident as 'pre-planned violent act of terrorism'. The Gujarat Minister of State for Home Gordhan Zadafia, then a trusted lieutenant of Modi and now a *bête noire,* said about forty people had been rounded up in connection with the attack on Sabarmati Express. He also volunteered to add that the incident could not be called communal violence "because there was no retaliation." In New Delhi, the Union Cabinet met for two hours in the night to take stock of the situation. The then Prime Minister Atal Bihari Vajpayee spoke to Chief Minister over phone and asked him to "firmly deal with the situation." The then Union Home Minister L.K. Advani also spoke to Modi. The Centre sounded a country-wide alert and directed the states to take suitable measures to maintain peace.

The gravity of the situation could be well understood as the Prime Minister linked Godhra incident to the vexed temple issue. Vajpayee asked the VHP to suspend its Ayodhya campaign of March 15 (2002), when it wanted to organise a *Shila Pujan.*

In the meantime, the charred bodies of the Godhra victims were brought to Ahmedabad. At Kalupur railway station in Ahmedabad, emotions ran high even as hours before at Godhra station when Modi inspected the charred compartment, reportedly an angry crowd including a few Bajrang Dal activists mobbed him. The message was getting clearer.

Giving their own signals about Hindu anger and possible retaliation, the VHP had called for a Bandh and issued a 24-hour deadline to the Government to bring the culprits to book.

Believing in eye for an eye theory, the Gujarat Hindus were looking for the opportune time to settle the 'score against Muslims', as many activists later said. State machinery including police turned blind and VHP and Bajrang Dal activists virtually took charge of the streets in communally hyper-sensitive Ahmedabad, the state's commercial hub and the popular traders' paradise. Here came Modi's role as the Chief Minister and the need to do his duty in protecting the 'Raj Dharma' (ethics of governance). It is supposed to be these failures on the part of the Chief Minister that is being used against him even now.

Senior Police Officer Sanjiv Bhatt, whose wife contested on Congress ticket unsuccessfully against Modi from Maninagar in December 2012 polls, has accused the Chief Minister of complicity in the post-Godhra riots of 2002. This has now snowballed into a major legal battle with the arrest of Bhatt and later his release after a fierce legal tussle.

About 80 people, majority of them Muslims and mostly from Ahmedabad, were killed on the first day of insane rage.

In one of the worst ever communal clashes, Hindu men and women also took to the streets, looting shops and renowned showrooms. Hotels and other business establishments owned by Muslims were ransacked and burnt. Twenty-six towns in the state were placed under curfew as arsonists took law into their hands with police mostly looking the other side. In a somewhat clear testimony of instructions from the very top—of course subject to be proved in a court of law—the police force had almost disappeared. Even traffic police personnel were not to be seen. Mass massacre took place at several places—two places prominent of them being Gulbarg Society in Chamanpura area and the minority-stronghold Naroda Patiya. Among others, former Congress MP Ehsan Jafri was charred to death by 2,000-strong mob in Gulbarg Society despite the politician reported to have called up police and his politician friends including the Chief Minister.

Jafri's wife Zakia had moved the Supreme Court and wanted Modi to be chargesheeted. The Apex Court has now said that everything related to the case must be settled in the trial court.

Ultimately on December 26, 2013, the trial court gave Modi a clean chit.

In a major relief for BJP's prime ministerial candidate, metropolitan magistrate B.J. Ganatra rejected the protest petition filed by Zakia Jafri, wife of late Congress MP Ehsan Jafri, against the clean chit given to Modi and others by the Special Investigation Team (SIT).

BJP spokesman Prakash Javadekar said, "Verdict sey ek muhar lag gayi ... Modiji key nirdosh hone par" (this verdict has put a stamp of approval to Narendra Modi's innocence).

"... there was hate campaign for more than a decade on the basis of complete falsehood. The court verdict giving clean chit to Narendra Modi is a welcome verdict and nails the falsehood in the bud," Javadekar had said.

In his characteristic style, Modi reacted assertively, saying 'Satyameva Jayate' (truth alone triumphs), first in a twitter message and the next day wrote a lengthy blog piece:

My dear sisters and brothers,

The law of nature is that Truth alone triumphs—Satyameva Jayate. Our judiciary having spoken, I felt it important to share my inner thoughts and feelings with the nation at large.

The end brings back memories of the beginning. The devastating earthquake of 2001 had plunged Gujarat into the gloom of death, destruction and sheer helplessness. Hundreds of lives were lost. Lakhs were rendered homeless. Entire livelihoods were destroyed. In such traumatic times of unimaginable suffering, I was given the responsibility to soothe and rebuild. And we had whole-heartedly plunged ourselves into the challenge at hand.

Within a mere five months, however, the mindless violence of 2002 had dealt us another unexpected blow. Innocents were killed. Families rendered helpless. Property built through years of toil destroyed. Still struggling to get back on its feet from the natural devastation, this was a crippling blow to an already shattered and hurting Gujarat.

I was shaken to the core. 'Grief', 'Sadness', 'Misery', 'Pain', 'Anguish', 'Agony'—mere words could not capture the absolute emptiness one felt on witnessing such inhumanity.

On one side was the pain of the victims of the earthquake, and on the other the pain of the victims of the riots. Indecisively confronting this great turmoil, I had to single-mindedly focus all the strength given to me by the almighty, on the task of peace, justice and rehabilitation; burying the pain and agony I was personally wracked with.

During those challenging times, I often recollected the wisdom in our scriptures; explaining how those sitting in positions of power did not have the right to share their own pain and anguish. They had to suffer it in solitude. I lived through the same, experiencing this anguish in searingly sharp intensity. In fact, whenever I remember those agonizing days, I have only one earnest prayer to God. That never again should such cruelly unfortunate days come in the lives of any other person, society, state or nation.

This is the first time I am sharing the harrowing ordeal I had gone through in those days at a personal level.

However, it was from these very built up emotions that I had appealed to the people of Gujarat on the day of the Godhra train burning itself; fervently urging for peace and restraint to ensure lives of innocents were not put at risk. I had repeatedly reiterated the same principles in my daily interactions with the media in those fateful days of February-March 2002 as well; publicly underlining the political will as well as moral responsibility of the government to ensure peace, deliver justice and punish all guilty of violence. You will also find these deep emotions in my recent words at my Sadbhavna Fasts, where I had emphasized how such deplorable incidents did not behove a civilized society and had pained me deeply.

In fact, my emphasis has always been on developing and emphasizing a spirit of unity; with the now widely used concept of 'my 5 crore Gujarati brothers and sisters' having crystallised right at the beginning of my tenure as CM itself from this very space.

However, as if all the suffering was not enough, I was also accused of the death and misery of my own loved ones, my Gujarati brothers and sisters. Can you imagine the inner turmoil and shock of being blamed for the very events that have shattered you!

For so many years, they incessantly kept up their attack, leaving no stone unturned. What pained even more was that in their over-zealousness to hit at me for their narrow personal and political ends, they ended up maligning my entire state and country. This heartlessly kept reopening the wounds that we were sincerely trying to heal. It ironically also delayed the very justice that these people claimed to be fighting for. Maybe they did not realize how much suffering they were adding to an already pained people.

Gujarat however had decided its own path. We chose peace over violence. We chose unity over divisiveness. We chose goodwill over hatred. This was not easy, but we were determined to commit for the long haul. From a life of daily uncertainty and fear; my Gujarat transformed into one of *Shanti, Ekta* and *Sadbhavna*. I stand a satisfied and reassured man today. And for this, I credit each and every Gujarati.

The Gujarat Government had responded to the violence more swiftly and decisively than ever done before in any previous riots in the country. Yesterday's judgement culminated a process of unprecedented scrutiny closely monitored by the highest court of the land, the Honourable Supreme Court of India. Gujarat's 12 years of trial by the fire have finally drawn to an end. I feel liberated and at peace.

I am truly grateful to all those who stood by me in these trying times; seeing through the facade of lies and deceit. With this cloud of misinformation firmly dispelled, I will now also hope that the many others out there trying to understand and connect with the real Narendra Modi would feel more empowered to do so.

Those who derive satisfaction by perpetuating pain in others will probably not stop their tirade against me. I do not expect them to. But, I pray in all humility, that they at least now stop irresponsibly maligning the 6 crore people of Gujarat.

Emerging from this journey of pain and agony; I pray to God that no bitterness seeps into my heart. I sincerely do not see this judgement as a personal victory or defeat, and urge all—my friends and especially my opponents—to not do so as well. I was driven by this same principle at the time of the Honourable Supreme Court's 2011 judgement on this matter. I fasted 37 days for *Sadbhavna*, choosing to translate the positive judgement into constructive action, reinforcing Unity and *Sadbhavna* in society at large.

I am deeply convinced that the future of any society, state or country lies in harmony. This is the only foundation on which progress and prosperity can be built. Therefore, I urge one and all to join hands in working towards the same, ensuring smiles on each and every face.

Once again, Satyameva Jayate!

Vande Mataram!

Narendra Modi (December 27, 2013)

Politically what remains to be analysed is what does the court verdict mean for Modi and BJP?

In fact, the quickest reaction from senior BJP leader Arun Jaitley, a known Narendra Modi confidant, within minutes the verdict from Ahmedabad metropolitan court gave relief to the Gujarat chief minister on Gulbarg society massacre case was: "Modi goes into the 2014 campaign untainted by propaganda."

This one-line reaction precisely summed up the paradox the saffron party is in *vis-a-vis* their latest mascot and prime ministerial candidate, Modi. Later at a press conference, Jaitley was again too apt to say that the judgement "is a moral victory for both Modi and the BJP."

The entire 'Modi-as-PM candidate' phenomenon *vis-a-vis* the legal hurdle with regard to 2002 riots (including Gulbarg case) always hung as 'the sword of Damocles' over Modi's head.

Braving the hyped campaign of the pro-Modi camp; a sizeable section of BJP leaders were always sceptical that 'brand Modi' has an inherent limitation. The refrain being Modi's alleged 'dangai' (riot-hit) face of 2002 will prevent non-NDA, non-UPA parties to move closer to BJP in the event the numbers do not make it near the magic figure of 272.

"The untouchable politics being pursued by a section of secularists against Modi will now stand defeated. We are hopeful, the verdict giving clean chit to Modi will be a big booster to NDA," said a senior party leader.

Several other leaders also see this as a removal of a major legal hurdle for Modi on way to winning allies and ultimately become Prime Minister.

Only a few days back, the Modi camp got a relief as Amit Shah's name was dropped from CBI chargesheet on Ishrat Jahan case.

Another party leader said the ruling showed that Congress party and other elements like Congress-friendly NGOs having vested interest wanted to 'subvert' the Modi government by prosecuting him and other Gujarat government officials.

"Those who have faith in the constitution feel relieved that the verdict has completely rooted out the serious allegations," the party leader said. Jaitley echoed similar sentiment saying, "a charge was made against Gujarat government that it was responsible for the conspiracy behind the riots. The truth is otherwise."

He said the Congress and so-called secular brigade have ignored the facts that the total number of persons arrested both for preventive and punitive actions in Gujarat for 2002 mayhem was 1,00,488. "This is more than the number of persons arrested in any other caste or religious tension in India. This negates the allegation of police connivance."

Jaitley also contended that Modi has only 'emerged stronger' having braved the serious legal hurdle. "The SIT had given a clean chit to Modi, today he got a stamp from the court," he remarked.

However, the division in BJP over accepting the court ruling still persisted as known Modi-detractors in the saffron party--the likes of Sushma Swaraj and her mentor L.K. Advani did not react in first couple of hours.

It may be recalled on September 12, 2011, when the Supreme Court had given a reprieve to Modi, the BJP patriarch Advani was quick to jump to the conclusion that the court verdict had given "a crushing reply to all those who vilified and maligned Modi for almost 10 long years."

Earlier in 2011, the Supreme Court has not ordered filing any chargesheet against the Chief Minister.

In fact, the first day of arson, 28th February 2002 was only like a tip of the iceberg as the arson and communal killings continued for weeks. Ahmedabad appeared a wilderness of pain and heartbreak. It was difficult to confirm the casualty figures by journalists even from police control rooms as pressure was telling on the cops manning both the city control room at Shahibaugh and the state control room at Gandhinagar. Almost 27 towns and cities spread over 16 districts were placed under curfew. There was a steady stream of injured people including women and children, coming to Ahmedabad's hospitals, mostly with burn injuries, stab injuries and sprinkles out of blasts of crude bombs.

On February 28, as mass killing of Muslims was engineered allegedly by Hindu chauvinists in the name of seeking justice to Godhra killings, two senior ministers sat in police control rooms in Ahmedabad and Gandhinagar. The then Gujarat Health Minister Ashok Bhatt, now deceased, who also had certain charges against him, was provided access to police control room at Commissioner's office at Shahibaugh in Ahmedabad, while Urban Development Minister and the then cabinet spokesman I.K. Jadeja, also a trusted lieutenant of Chief Minister Modi, had parked himself in state police control room at Gandhinagar for about four hours. The then Ahmedabad Police Commissioner P.C. Pandey later tried to make a defence of the entire episode saying the ministers were allowed access to the control rooms to 'facilitate' easy flow of government directions. It was for the first time, that any communal and ethnic conflict was marred by gross abuse of official position and documents—like voters' list and traders' licenses. There was enough indication that a 'distinct pattern' of communal cleansing was carried out against Muslims, not sparing the women and children, especially in Ahmedabad and adjacent places.

However, in Ahmedabad even months after the riots, the local residents apparently showed approval for the violence and arson against the Muslims who were attacked irrespective of their economic status and profession.

Several hotels and eateries even with secular names like 'Kabir' and 'Millennium' were damaged. Even business establishments run by Muslims in partnership with Hindus were attacked. The message for Hindus in Ahmedabad and Gujarat who had befriended Muslims was perhaps clear—do not do business with 'meat eaters'.

"Loot was carried out driven by greed but there was an added refrain that they were looting the properties of the Muslims," lamented Rafiqa Bano of riot-hit Naroda Patiya—whose four children were killed and one daughter seriously injured in a blaze. There was also active participation of women from middle class Hindu families.

With such high rate of undiluted approval of anti-Muslim violence from the Hindus, one humble understanding is obvious that such merciless killings and the loot could take place only on a soil 'fertile' with religious prejudices. Godhra and the post-Godhra ghosts would, therefore, haunt Gujarat and its people for a long time.

It is not without good reason that RSS veteran M.G. Vaidya, though unapologetic about the violence, told a news conference in Mumbai in August 2002, that the post-Godhra violence was "unlike a Hindu way of reaction." But these were the processes of creating the brand equity in Modi. All subsequent polls, the 2002, 2007 and 2012 assembly elections in Gujarat were treated as plebiscite on him and the BJP gamble paid. He is truly the poster boy of the party; though with a latent riddle. A letter to the Editor in the periodical *The Sunday Indian* rightly commented that the 2012 Gujarat Assembly elections had taken Modimania to a new hysterical level.

Coming back to the 2002 incidents, the arsonists even razed the tomb of one of the best-known Urdu poets of the state—Vali Gujarati. Many small shrines in the city were also destroyed during the frenzy that rocked Ahmedabad. At Shahibaugh, a stone's throw from city Police Commissioner's office, rioters demolished Vali Gujarati's tomb and a Hanuman shrine reportedly built over it promptly.

The anti-Muslim incidents had a 'salutary effect' in uniting the Hindus. Such unity in a caste-ridden Hindu society in Gujarat was no mean achievement for the believers of Hindutva. Modi was strongly regarded as someone who stood by the Hindus and thus, in no time, he emerged a local hero and Sangh Parivar propagandists rightly called him *Hindu Hridayasamrat*.

Thus, as police and administration went blind even as the VHP and Sangh activists virtually took charge of the state, the Hindutva elements seemed quite emboldened by the backing they got. The confidence swelled into such height that the arsonists did not hesitate even to burn the offices of the Wakf Board and the Minority Finance Corporation located in the supposed-to-be 'high-security' Secretariat area in the state's seat of power and authority—Gandhinagar.

Brandishing swords and sticks, Bajrang Dal activists and other Hindu youths at many places screamed aloud that they were seeking justice and revenge for the 'well-planned' attack on *Ram Bhakts* in Godhra. Thousands of arsonists went on the rampage torching shops, Muslim colonies and public property in both urban and rural areas across the state.

The polarization of Hindu voters suited Modi—no doubt—but the manner and the speed with which it came, even Modi was left surprised. According to some police and administrative reports, the Gujarat Government thought the retaliation could go on maximum for 72 hours; that is three days. But it went for three months. "Modi had to justify the reaction of the majority voters. This endeared him to Hindus irrespective of caste factors", commented one retired State Government employee in November 2007.

On the other hand, as pointed out in the book *Modi to Moditva: An Uncensored Truth*, "Modi could be singled out and even now there are groups and individuals within BJP who are singling him out for the 2002 holocaust. But one could have throughout given the Gujarat Chief Minister the benefit of doubt. After all, he had replaced Keshubhai Patel, when BJP was at the receiving end of the electorate's anger. The BJP expected him to deliver Gujarat; and Modi did it like a true batting star of a limited overs game in a one-day cricket fashion—mustered the runs little bothering about playing unorthodox shots."

CASTE UNITY

Speaking from Sangh Parivar point of view, the RSS-BJP-VHP triangular axis of the Sangh Parivar had succeeded in mobilizing unity of purpose within caste-ridden Hindus in Gujarat. This is no small achievement for the Parivar in Gujarat as according to a *Bombay Gazetteer*, "Gujarat was pre-eminently a land of castes. In 1827, there were as many as 207 castes in the city of Surat alone which did not marry outside their community," says *Gazetteer of Bombay Presidency* edited by British scholar James Campbell and published in 1901.

Interaction with social analysts and academicians even after 10 years since the riots reveal that the Hindu mobilization was made possible due to the Ayodhya movement and it only gained momentum with each communal backlash since 1969, followed by 1985 and post-Babri Masjid demolition in 1992.

In many localities in 2002 during riot-torn days, even those from backward communities and *Dalits* in Gujarat spoke the language and verb of Uma Bhartis, Ashok Singhals and Bal Thackerays.

It is significant to note that during the post-Godhra retaliation, the right wing Hindu leadership also won the support of *Dalits* and OBCs—especially the upwardly mobile strata in 1995 and 1998 assembly polls when BJP banked on slogans like *Ram Mandir banana hai* and *Abki Bari Atal Bihari.*

The absence of third political force of caste-based leadership like Mayawati or Mulayam Singh Yadav was another factor that played a catalytic role in endearing the OBC and *Dalit* Hindus close to the Sangh Parivar and the BJP in Gujarat, rightly dubbed as the 'Hindutva laboratory'. Therefore, despite facing decades of negligence and deprivation from the upper castes, the backward castes joined ranks with majority Hindus and took to the streets in the name of Hindu revivalism. It is a vital aspect of the society in Gujarat which needs deeper studies that how despite ascendancy of caste identity consciousness and V.P. Singh's post-Mandal politics sweeping northern India, the communal polarization continued to exist between Hindus and Muslims.

It is coincident that Modi has emerged a neo-champion of the Hindutva cause since 2002. In effect, all the hard work for Hindu polarization was led by the then Keshubhai Patel-led BJP Government's tenure in tandem with influential VHP. The 'one Hindu' slogan of VHP was well-propagated by BJP. It had cemented the campaign of undivided identity of the Hindus despite the caste divisions. Local RSS office-bearers in Ahmedabad often refer to the former Chief Minister Keshubhai Patel's comment to a lower caste youth in Mehsana district during a RSS camp in 2001; "If you are a Harijan, I am a Harijan too. And if I am Patel, you are also Patel because we both are Hindus."

Now, look at the irony, in 2012 December polls; the same Keshubhai Patel's Gujarat Parivartan Party was badly humbled even in Saurashtra, supposed to be his fiefdom for decades. On the other hand, no one in Gujarat asked about Modi's caste. Therefore, it is not without good reason that after the results came in on December 20, 2012; Modi reportedly told BJP chief spokesman Ravi Shankar Prasad, "Please tell the media that my own caste (Ganchi) constitutes only about one lakh voters in Gujarat."

For Gujarat watchers again, interestingly, pragmatism of highly entrepreneur community, Vanias, has left other communities, including the Hindu backward castes, in the entire state, highly impressed.

Vanias form only 5-6 per cent of the population of the state. They are scattered throughout the state and thanks to their business acumen and economic success, their culture has virtually become 'synonymous' with Gujarati culture and perhaps also for those non-Gujaratis settled in Gujarat. The backward castes, bereft of any leader like Mayawati or Lalu Yadav, therefore, look forward to the trading class Vanias and to some extent to Rajputs and Brahmins and automatically follow the religious or for that matter, the communal lines of these communities. Thus, in the ultimate analysis we see that it is more than sheer coincidence that Modi has not only justified the Hindu anger and the subsequent violence in the state.

Days after the senseless violence, mostly targeting the minority Muslims, the Gujarat Chief Minister was in no tune to express regrets for the killings. He had spoken about the five crore Gujaratis (and by 2012 six crore) and in September 2011 made it amply clear, "whatever I do, I do for the entire population."

In a decisive mandate in 2002 which virtually ensured that Gujarat could be drenched in saffron, in Saurashtra region, where polarization was said to be minimal and Patels were said to be annoyed with the saffron party for dumping Keshubhai Patel, BJP maintained its dominance, bagging 37 of 52 seats. It swept aside Congress in Rajkot district, bagging 9 out of 11 seats while making significant inroads into the traditional Congress bastion of central Gujarat. It picked up 41 out of 43 seats in the region. BJP also surged ahead in Northern region and tribal belts of Panchmahal and Dahod showing post-Godhra riots had sought to bring even tribals under the influence of Hindutva influence. The Modi brand had truly arrived in its full steam.

For next five years or for that matter, the subsequent years till circa 2012, the story of Gujarat is synonymous with the story of its Chief Minister. Neither internal dissensions within the party nor any other issue has even for one day threatened Modi's undisputed position as the topmost leader of Gujarat.

Therefore, we also see that the Modi-brand is essentially a qualitative Hindutva brand. No wonder, even at his *Sadbhavna* or goodwill fast in September 2011, there was no ventilation of remorse or apology from Modi for the 2002 riots. It's said and not without good reason that politicians do everything considering their electoral strategy. Going by this rationale, an apology could come from a *neta* only if there is a "damaged relationship between a politician and his voters."

In Modi's case, the relationship with his support base has not been damaged. Rather it has emerged a stronger bond since the riots as he is regarded largely as the only Chief Minister who stood by the majority Hindus, said to be waiting for justice for decades *vis-a-vis* the assertive politics of Muslims till 2002.

"For Brand Modi, it's the relationship with those who do not vote for him which is on the rocks and therefore, why should he really bother about it," explained one senior retired intelligence official, who served in Gujarat.

In other words, 88 per cent Hindus are backing Modi to the hilt and it will perhaps only be a political harakiri if he tenders an apology for the 2002 misadventure in not acting against the alleged Hindu rioters. Thus, the 'Modi Brand' today cannot see beyond Hindutva plank and none other than Modi himself knows it pretty well.

"He is more an ear-to-the-ground politician. Look at the way Advani tried to come out of his Hindutva poster-boy image by his remarks on secular Jinnah; he left his traditional Hindu vote base shaken and hardly benefited among Muslims," the intelligence official argued eloquently.

However, the *Sadbhavna* fast launched in September 2011 and rather taken into rural areas of Gujarat was definitely aimed towards 're-branding of Modi'. But it was not directed to turn 'secular' overnight as Advani's misadventure was a lesson for Modi too. Instead, Modi projected his brand equity as a 'developmental model'. How much of that had impacted the voters' mind, well the mandate 2012 in Gujarat and later the assembly elections in 2013 speak for themselves.

Modi's determination to stay put his core constituency, the hardliner Hindutva, is somewhat able to make the impact as his political honesty. So much is his acceptability even among non-resident Indians that in 2007 after the assembly polls, Shreyas Suresh, wrote in his blog from Chicago: "Recent Indian political history has seen a decline of strong and honest leaders. Modi is one of the last remaining few. People might call him an authoritarian, but the need of the moment is just that. He has not only turned Gujarat into a model state with terrific development but also given the people a corruption free government." In 2011, one 15-year-old youngster from Assam said, Modi to her was like a 'benevolent dictator' who needs to rule India with decisiveness and strong hands.

All these years Modi has been very tactful too. He is constantly playing as someone dealing with an uncooperative Central Government headed by Congress-led coalition. So his repeated attempts are to play the central ill-treatment meted to non-Congress states.

Over these years, nursing the clear ambition to become the BJP's Prime Ministerial candidate, Modi has possibly been able to reinvent himself to gain wider acceptability. It is perhaps with this issue in mind that in 2011 his poster was put up at Ahmedabad Airport, albeit for the first time, to wish good luck to the Haj pilgrims. Clearly determined to ensure that the minority community does not upset his electoral prospects, both in 2012 assembly polls and 2014 Lok Sabha polls; for the first time, Modi and several other BJP leaders have reached out to Haj pilgrims. In October 2011, huge hoardings showing saffron leaders wishing pilgrims 'Haj

Mubarak' were displayed at the Ahmedabad airport. Modi's poster showed not only the Chief Minister waving at the pilgrims but also requested them to pray for Gujarat's development. In the past, only Haj Committee members were seen on the posters.

Ilyas Qureshi, spokesman for Ahmedabad city unit of Congress, tried to answer the puzzle well. "Our understanding is that Modi has tried to play safe. Fielding all Hindu candidates is on expected line for his voters here. Modi just got scared that fielding Muslims would have irked Hindu voters. Then, he would have been a bigger loser," he said.

Another contention among political watchers was that the Keshubhai Patel-led Gujarat Parivartan Party (GPP) had also perhaps forced BJP to stick to Modi's hardliner stance. "It goes without saying that GPP led by Keshubhai is actually more a hardliner outfit. It has the likes of Gordhan Zadafia, the Home Minister in Modi Government in 2002. My understanding is that Modi must have feared GPP factor and thus decided not to field Muslim candidates even if he wanted to," said one Dr. Ejaz Qazi from Jamalpur.

However, BJP's new found Muslim face, Asifa Khan denied such compulsions. "Fielding Muslims or not should not be made a parameter of deciding whether Muslims are with Modi or not. If GPP is a factor, they would have influenced recent panchayat and taluka level votes too," said Asifa, once a close aide of senior Congress leader Ahmed Patel and had recently deserted Congress to join BJP. "Winnability is always of paramount importance when you decide about tickets. BJP cannot make an exception just to make some symbolic gestures. UP has 69 Muslim MLAs, do you suggest Muslims are having only a great time in Uttar Pradesh. Muslims in Gujarat want to move ahead, they want to be part of inclusive development of Modi," she had maintained. But even among BJP supporters and party's foot-soldiers, "not to put any Muslim candidate was a calculative political strategy. Politics in Gujarat is different. Yes, it is polarized and so Modi cannot leave the hardcore Hindutva plank which made him what he is," says 50-year-old Anurag Patel, who had gathered at BJP candidate Amit Shah's street corner meeting at Narayanpura assembly constituency.

At one end, Modi's hypnotic oratorical skill and theatrical flair—for instance the 'Mia Musharraf' rhetoric and *hum panch hamare pachis*—are forcing critics to lambast him. Others find in him glimpses of Singapore's Lee Kuan Yew, who once famously spoke about the need for trade between democracy and discipline. For Modi, it's a right balance of hardliner Hindu chauvinism and development. In the ultimate though, it's the *Moditva*—that remains his lasting legacy.

However, it ought to be stated that Modi needs to be careful in pursuing his ambitions for a nationwide acceptability and ultimately emerge winner as BJP's, or for that matter NDA's PM candidate. But Modi knows the art and politics of the survival with Hindutva politics too well. He has been very careful and thus not going to overstep as was done by Kalyan Singh once. By over-estimating his own strengths and taking on Vajpayee personally, Kalyan Singh had actually written his political obituary and brought in immense damage to BJP in Uttar Pradesh.

Even the party stalwart and the original Hindutva mascot L.K. Advani had to struggle hard to retain his position as the leader of the party after his Jinnah-remark harakiri. As a matter of fact, Advani also stood isolated after 2005 Jinnah-secular misadventure and he had to ultimately give up BJP presidentship and after 2009 poll debacle, the Leader of the Opposition post. In fact, even others like Balraj Madhok had to bite the dust once he was shown the doors by the Sangh Parivar fountainhead, the RSS.

But those who know Modi maintain that he knows the size of his *chadar* (read shoes). Anyone different from Modi's personality would have found it extremely difficult to survive the manner he has managed the tight-rope walking. This naive sense of understanding the ground politics, undoubtedly, keeps him going.

Years back, former Nagaland Chief Minister who also served as Himachal Pradesh Governor, Hokishe Sema, known as the protagonist of nationalism among the few pro-India Naga leaders, had said that the Indian political system over the years generally prescribed for *status quo*. An atmosphere would always be created wherein individual aspirations and 'out-of-the-box' thinking would be strongly resisted.

After making a closer scrutiny of Gujarat politics and Modi's approach to it, we are tempted here to maintain that Modi's politics perhaps brings that different genre.

Going back to Naga leader Hokishe Sema's diagnosis of the Indian polity; it is a fact that to survive and thrive in a political atmosphere that Modi inherited, especially after post-2002 riots and highly successful election, one needs to have some peculiar qualities. Modi has in him that combined magic box of naive understanding, trust in some hardliner ideology, willingness to manipulate things and an astute sense of humour and importantly, the timing.

The theatrical perfection—of 'Mia Musharraf' rhetoric and *hum panch hamare pachis* lines; his timely decision in 2012 polls not to field any Muslim candidate, have added to his electoral support base and also the overall public image.

In the run up to the 2012 assembly polls, there were sustained efforts by a section of BJP in Gujarat—at least on face value—ostensibly with the backing of the Chief Minister himself to present a 'moderate' and 'accommodating' face of Hindutva champion Narendra Modi towards Muslims.

However, notwithstanding strong indications dropped earlier at various levels that the saffron party could field a few Muslim candidates—albeit as an 'image makeover' attempt for Modi, the saffron party yet again declined to oblige the battered minority community. Critics perceived that by doing so perhaps, Modi had missed a big picture. But as the results made it clear, Modi was bang on target. BJP could even pick up an essentially Muslim-predominant Jamalpur-Khadia seat in Ahmedabad.

The Jamalpur-Khadia seat was created out of merger of Muslim-dominated Jamalpur and Hindu-dominated Khadia. But put together 'Jamalpur Khadia' has an electorate of over 1.80 lakh voters with an overwhelming more than 1 lakh Muslims. The punters had hoped that even BJP could field Muslims and in fact had zeroed down on two local leaders A.I. Sayed and Abdul Faqir. But the saffron party had chosen to field Bhushan Bhatt, son of Late Ashok Bhatt, who used to represent known Hindutva citadel Khadia 6 times. "Our understanding is that Modi has tried to play safe," said Ilyas Qureshi, spokesman for Ahmedabad city unit Congress.

One likes it or not; knowing very well that he is a loner in the game—and more so if he is on the top—Modi is creditably displaying personal commitment to achieve the excellence in his career and improve his performance as a Chief Minister, who delivers. In the run up to the 2012 polls, even his worst detractors could not help agreeing that Modi's image before the electorate was as a 'doer', a tough leader who can command, take decision and much importantly against whom there are no corruption charges.

"With these qualities in his kitty, even Muslim voters and a few Congress opponents in the state admitted that the stains of 2002 riots only looked a humble apology," commented Delhi-based magazine *Power Politics* edited by a senior journalist Hari Jaisingh.

His detractors in Congress and the scores of NGO activists said there was hardly any effective development and Modi has only created a 'smokescreen' about it. "In last decade Modi government has made an aura of development and fooled the people," said GPCC Chief Arjun Modhwadia.

But the turnout of historical 70 per cent of electorate and the BJP vote share revolving around 49 per cent—a clear difference of about 8 per cent with Congress—only pricked the balloon of such a campaign.

Modi's officials admire him for his gruelling attention to details—when he ensures getting complete information about an issue or a person he has to confront; on the other hand, he is a tested hand in macro-management also. The strong sense of self-confidence has also made him ruthless, like the manner he denied the ticket to the late Haren Pandya for 2002 assembly elections braving the entire party leadership including Atal Bihari Vajpayee. Yet again, in 2011, he was uneasy with party president Nitin Gadkari reinstating his *bête noire* Sanjay Joshi. He also displayed the tenacity in handling Pravin Togadia and the clinical precision he applied to sideline the one-time vocal VHP leader.

Modi's best time is perhaps yet to come. But Modi does a good balance between his strengths and the possible areas of problems he could face while dealing with some issues. For instance, he did not hesitate to take the first step in clearing the ambiguity over his supposed differences with L.K. Advani. On November 7, 2011, a day after former Deputy Prime Minister's 6th *Rath Yatra* entered Gujarat, Modi sought to clarify that there was no difference between him and his mentor Advani. Even in September 2013, when he was crowned party's PM-candidate brushing aside L.K. Advani's reservation, he did not miss the opportunity to walk into Advani's residence for an audience with the party veteran.

On January 27, 2012, the newsletter from Swarnim

Gujarat claimed that in a survey spread across 19 states, as many as 24 per cent of respondents had favoured Modi as the Prime Minister as against the 17 per cent of his closest competitor Rahul Gandhi. It maintained that Modi's standing has improved from 9 per cent in August 2010 and 12 per cent in January 2011.

Under him even the worst of critics have to agree that the state of Gujarat is growing faster than any state. "... 10 years on (since the carnage) whilst the controversy (2002 riots) is still being debated, it isn't stopping business from flowing in (Gujarat)", said BBC in its report on the eve of the completion of 10 years of the country's worst religious violence.

In terms of his re-branding *vis-a-vis* as a 'development Chief Minister'; observers feel the single-most right thing happening in Gujarat under Modi is that the business and industry are treated with priority. There is no lip-service or politics of shifting a matter by passing the buck to certain excuses or as they say, bureaucratic bottlenecks. Instead, all commitments made by Modi have been served to the industry. At least the entire apparatus seemed to be busy delivering the goods.

The 'Modi brand' has paradoxically also caught the Congress in quite a quagmire-like situation. In January 2012, Sonia Gandhi's outfit launched a satire-advertisement but the same proved counter-productive. The advertisement had listed the achievements of all the Chief Ministers in Gujarat since 1960 to prove the point that Modi was "not the sole claimant of all the credits", as reported in *The Hindu*.

Though the Congress leaders said the advertisement was 'a satire' but the message ended up saying that "the Chief Minister Modi was a master organiser and astute election strategist". The Congress managers maintained that the party only intended to 'mock' at Modi's towering and most of the time highly misleading campaign that: even Narmada dam came during his time. The Gujarat Congress spokesman merely had said: "What we are trying to convey through the advertisement is that Gujarat's progress is not due to one person (that is Modi)."

In the subsequent chapters of this book, you will find how corporate honchos from across the board had lauded Modi.

Bombardier, the Canadian company, built a manufacturing plant in Savli, to bring out compartments for Delhi Metro in what is said to be a record 18 months. There are many others including Indian honchos Tatas and Ambanis. Thus, when it comes to his administration and encouragement to entrepreneurship, he is no longer hated.

The results are also showing, say Gujarat Government officials. In 2001, the year Modi took over office, Gujarat's economy shrank by 5 per cent and by 2011 state's Gross Domestic Product shot up to an annual 11 per cent. In yet another turning point to boost Gujarat's industrialization situation, on 29 October 2011 in New Delhi, auto-maker Maruti Suzuki's board meeting approved a new manufacturing facility in Gujarat and purchase of land in Mehsana district. The board "granted approval to purchase land in Mehsana district for future expansion of manufacturing facilities. This purchase would be subject to final negotiations on price and all legal formalities being completed", a company announcement said. This was after Maruti's plant faced labour related problems in Haryana. To Modi's credit, the energy companies Royal Dutch Shell and Total have opened a major liquid natural gas terminal in Gujarat and Indian Torrent Power has built a huge plant. Among others, Tata Motors, DuPont, General Motors, Hitachi and dozens of other foreign and Indian companies have built factories, expanded operations and invested in projects in the state. "If you are an investor in India, Gujarat must be at the top of your list", said one business leader of an American trade group at a Vibrant Gujarat meet.

In effect, the business houses including those from outside these days hardly bother about media campaign and constant allegations from his detractors about 2002 carnage and Modi's supposed RSS-agenda, the 'hate Muslim' philosophy. Both the overseas and Indian corporate honchos laud his quick delivery system.

In 2011, China's ambassador to India, Zhang Yan, reached out to Modi and expressed China's interest in working together to sharpen Gujarat's industrial and manufacturing edge. He also invited Modi to visit China, which the Chief Minister had accepted.

"The Chinese invitation to Modi is an astute political move and sends a very strong political signal, particularly in the context of the fact that Modi was in 2005 controversially denied a visa to travel to the US for his role in the 2002 riots on the strength of lobbying by human rights activists in the US", said a web newsletter from Gujarat—'GujaratIndia.com'

By rolling out the red carpet for Modi, in contrast to the US visa snub, Chinese officials are making a calculated investment in the future, which they know will be well-received by a leader who prides himself as an embodiment of Gujarati *asmita* (self-respect), it said. The Chinese made it clear that they are open to do business with him without offering lectures on human rights. For Chinese leaders, Modi's involvement in the 2002 riots and his response as an administrator since then, have parallels with a defining moment in Chinese history, apparently the 1989 massacre of students around the Tiananmen Square in Beijing.

Right after the 4th June 1989 crackdown, China faced international criticism and was subjected to sanctions. Foreign investors, who had been warming up to the China story after the first round of reforms unveiled by Deng Xiaoping in 1976, no longer wanted to be associated with a regime that had blood on its hands. It was a particularly grim moment for the Chinese Communist Party. Yet, Deng Xiaoping successfully changed the China narrative by unleashing a second round of reforms, which was the cue for investors to return, overlooking the taint of Tiananmen.

Similarly, Modi has managed in recent years to change the narrative about Gujarat away from the horrendous 2002 riots. No wonder, under Modi, Ahmedabad figures only behind two Chinese cities—Chengdu and Chongqing—on Forbes' list of 10 fastest-growing cities of the future.

In the words of Republican Congressman (from the United States) Joe Walsh, who represents Illinois' 8th district from the Chicago area, "Modi has been recognised across the world for his staunch stance against corruption and for making Gujarat a shining example of the success that pro-growth, limited Government policies can create. In the US's trying economic times, we could learn a great deal from him. Instead of denying him a visa, we should be inviting him to apply." (Interview with news agency IANS.)

Remarkably, Walsh had pointed out that the ban on Modi's visa was "not in compliance with the US law". He backed his allegation with observation that "Modi has never been tried nor convicted, as required under this statute, of any religious crimes in any country. Regardless, the statute states that he can be denied a visa only up to 24 months after a conviction. The allegations arose in 2002; it is now 2012."

Modi knows the art of management of electorate's mind pretty well. In 2007, he made a good synthesis of development mantra along with 'no appeasement' towards Muslims. He almost endorsed the questionable encounter of Sohrabuddin amid much media attacks and even vilification by rivals like Sonia Gandhi, who virtually called him a *maut ka saudagar* (merchant of death). It's altogether a different chapter that Modi had in fact benefited from such gross indiscriminate kind of remarks.

In the run up to the 2012 assembly polls, he talked about 'inclusive growth of Gujarat and Gujaratis'. The theme of his *Sadbhavna* Fast speech in September 2011 was, "I do nothing for minorities nor anything for majority (the Hindus)." His development card is for all Gujaratis, Modi emphasised.

As the senior journalist Prabhu Chawla says, "He (Modi) has ensured that he remained prime news on prime time for the most part of the year." If a newsmaker is to attain the immortality in the pages of history; among the Indian *neta* class, undoubtedly Modi would be at the top. Yet again, testing time came as an administrator too. When Tata's Nano project was hounded out of West Bengal in 2008, he knew there would be probable competitions among other states to accommodate Nano car factory.

On October 3, 2008 when Tata Motors announced that they would be moving out of Singur, Ratan Tata reportedly received letters of invitation from four states. But Modi sent in an SMS which simply said 'Welcome to Gujarat'.

Ratan Tata, Chairman, Tata Sons, later commented, "Narendra Modi promised me it would take a few days. And his few days meant only three days wherein in common business-administration parlance in any other state could mean at least couple of months minimum." Located 60 km from Ahmedabad, 1,100-acre plot in Sanand was passed on to Tata Motors by the Modi regime.

This piece of land where the Tata Motors' manufacturing unit came up in a record 14 months belonged to the Anand Agriculture University for over a century. In three days the Government acquired the land and passed it to Tatas and there were no protests or so.

Today, many other industrial houses also agree that Gujarat is most amenable to investment and industrial growth.

Even Mamata Banerjee, a former NDA ally and a minister under Vajpayee, almost stunned her friends and foes alike when she told a gathering of 85th Annual General Meeting of FICCI that "Gujarat has been nurtured and it is progressing." As political observers and journalists, everyone is watching Modi for over 2 decades now, sometime from close range, mostly during the last 10 years. In *Modi to Moditva: An Uncensored Truth,* Nirendra Dev has said. "There's a quirk of paradoxical twists in the tale about him (Modi). Just as we know about his 'Mia Musharraf' remarks especially in months immediately after the riots and in the run up to the 2002 polls, there is an element which draws somewhat parallelism between him and Parvez Musharraf. Like Musharraf, Modi too was extremely obsessed about his image—when he seized power, when he oversaw the turbulent 2002 days of arson and killings and in the later stage as he tried to give a 'façade' of developmental governance to his state. Those who have kept a closer observation on him, admit, that Modi wanted to present himself palatable (acceptable) to various constituencies without, however, compromising on his chief plank—the hardcore Hindutva. Like Musharraf remained ever defensive of military role, Modi too has never compromised on his image as the Hindutva poster boy.

Like Musharraf, Modi also has been trying to build up his image to the international community and has so far suitably made use of the development in the state pretty well—definitely surpassing the attempts made by Musharraf."

But it ought to be clarified that it would not be fair to label Modi as an image reflection of Musharraf. The former Pakistani ruler remained a pariah to most countries, Modi is somehow not. His Vintage Gujarat business summits are a pointer for the same as was his high-profile visit to China—essentially aimed to boost business.

The 'Vibrant Gujarat' has been successfully marketed as a major global business event every alternate year essentially to showcase the Chief Minister than perhaps the state. Nevertheless the impact is so profound that Modi's American lobbying and public relations firm, APCO Worldwide, also has bagged international awards for its work promoting the project.

So much is the aura or awe associated with Modi that many laurels coming from industry captains could even outdo the best of political sycophancy of the Congress or Mayawati cult.

On the summit in 2011, at the glittering function in Gandhinagar on January 12, 2011, the Reliance group Chairman Mukesh Ambani said, "Gujarat is emerging as a superpower of the 21st century under him." His brother Anil Ambani further said, "After Mahatma Gandhi, it is under the leadership of Modi that the state is seeing a phenomenal progress. My father Dhirubhai Ambani, after meeting Mr. Modi, had said he will go a long way." Tata group Chairman Ratan Tata too was all praise for the Chief Minister. "By your exemplary leadership, you are establishing new grounds in industrial development," he had said.

Officials in Gandhinagar say, the five summits since 2003 have generated investment pledges worth over $ 900 billion for Gujarat even as debate persists on how much money has really seen the ground of Gujarat and how much of it has been really transformed into projects. Nevertheless, on papers at least the 2011 show itself earned an assurance of over $ 450 billion.

By 2013 January end as yet another Vibrant Gujarat was hosted, among others Mukesh Ambani pledged a whopping investment of Rs. 1 lakh crore.

Politically, for Congress and his opponents within NDA and BJP, thus there is little to dispute that Modi makes a lethal combination of a Hindutva champion and an industry friendly development oriented leader. He and his admirers are rightly waiting for these to garner votes and assure Modi a place as the prime ministerial candidate for BJP and the BJP-led coalition, NDA.

3. Modi–The Vote Catcher

THE ELECTORAL SUCCESS STORY: WHAT MAKES MODI CLICK

In the run up the crucial December 2012 Assembly Elections in Gujarat, if there was one question that haunted everyone—from sceptical journalists to political rivals and even his colleagues in BJP—was: What really makes Narendra Modi click? Even the well-worn political theory of 'anti-incumbency' did not work against him.

But as the results poured in on December 20, one obvious factor that weighed in favour of the man of the moment—Narendra Modi—was his assertive approach. By refusing to be defeated he had in a sense emerged a winner long before the battle was over.

In fact, just hours before the results came in, he presided over a meeting of his last cabinet (of previous term) and gave final touches to the preparation for the Vibrant Gujarat Summit.

Not surprisingly, the Gujarati voters were charmed by his neo-assertive confidence as much by his brand equity

'Moditva'—as discussed earlier—essentially a fine synthesis of parochial Gujarati pride, Hindutva philosophy and the developmental trump card.

The marketing gurus were little perplexed that in the month-long campaign to the polls and even before that Modi, much maligned for the 2002 anti-Muslim carnage, had tried to project himself as a 'doer', a tough leader who can command and take decisions. That way he pitted himself in contest with Dr. Manmohan Singh in Delhi, whose weak-kneed approaches have left even strongest admirers anguished.

Much importantly there were no corruption charges against Modi. With these qualities in his kitty, even Muslim voters and a few Congress opponents in the state admitted that the stains of 2002 riots only looked a humble apology.

"The riot focus on this former RSS Pracharak has dissolved, just a bit, after the Supreme Court-appointed SIT recently gave Modi a clean chit in the post-Godhra Gulbarg massacre case," said magazine *The Sunday Indian*. M. Kumar, a reader wrote in his letter to the editor for magazine, more assertively: "...every great leader has certain weaknesses, which can be ignored because of his contributions. National leaders were responsible for anti-Sikh riots, Babri Masjid demolition, partition and the Kashmir problem. It does not mean that they were individually responsible for the problems ... Gujarat and the rest of the country need to move on."

Bagging 115 seats, just 2 short of 117 benchmark of 2007, braving the anti-incumbency of last decade and fighting almost single-handedly against all odds and hurdles thrown by apparently disgruntled RSS, VHP, Bajrang Dal and the armies of NGO activists besides the sustained campaign by Congress and a former BJP heavyweight Keshubhai; Modi has able to prove the obvious.

That way, the chief take-away from the mandate 2012 *vis-*

a-vis Modi, most vocal proponent of Hindutva, is: No matter how strong it is and how long it sustains, the storm actually ends one day.

Truly, there is no denying the fact that Modi's legion of powerful critics is a force to reckon with. Besides an entire industry of human right activists, the NGOs, the likes of Shabnam Hashmi, who temporarily even joined Congress formally, and controversial cop Sanjiv Bhatt (who fielded his wife Shweta against Modi on Congress ticket) and hyped judicial activism—Modi had to brave through all.

Modi's benefactor for long years, L.K. Advani, is absolutely right when he says he is yet to find a politician who is more vilified than Modi.

Modi is seen as a combination of Hitler, Nero, Mussolini and Franco. The VHP foot-soldiers, BJP's original workforce in Hindu laboratory Gujarat, were told to work against him.

But Modi has braved through all hurdles. In concrete terms, while several Congress bigwigs GPCC chief Modhwadia and leader of the opposition in the last assembly Shaktisinh Gohil lost, significantly enough BJP could pick up Muslim-dominated Jamalpur-Khadia assembly segment in Ahmedabad city. This is a rare occasion in recent history when Jamalpur's Muslim voters have backed a saffron candidate.

Modi was personally comfortable in Maninagar while Keshubhai Patel's lieutenant Gordhan Zadafia lost in Gondal.

Both 'symbolic' candidates Shweta Bhatt (suspended cop Sanjiv Bhatt's wife) against Modi in Maninagar and Jagrutiben Pandya, widow of late Haren Pandya in Ellisbridge also lost.

In Maninagar, a Sikh entrepreneur, actually summed it up better: "Agar Manmohan Singh bhi ladhchhe ... toh bhi mein BJP na mata pachhu" (even if Manmohan Singh contests against Modi, I will vote for BJP only).

BJP too had losers like Dilip Sanghani – Amreli and Jay Narayan Vyas in Sidhapur while former Home Minister Amit Shah, once arrested for encounter case, romped home in Naranpura.

GPP chief and former BJP satrap Keshubhai Patel won Visavadar, so did Shankersinh Vaghela of Congress. However, BJP rebel and who fought against Nirma Cement Kanubhai Kalsariya lost in Gariyadhar.

What made Modi click? Modi's image in the ultimate has been pro-development also pro-urban youth – a certain contrast with a 'weak' Manmohan Singh or even mofussil casteist Keshubhai Patel.

The 'performer' factor in terms of governance, Modi tried to use BJP foot-soldiers if not large section of his party colleagues, firmly believe will be a catch-point to encash *vis-a-vis* the leadership of Dr. Manmohan Singh or Rahul Gandhi at the national level. Actually, the Congress remains clueless completely and the 'Chintan Shivir' the party held in Congress could not arrive at any success on that score. It was perhaps because of this the Congress strategy remained ambiguous and confused – from Sonia Gandhi's plain speaking about loss of traditional vote bank, blatant sycophancy for Rahul and then the 'saffron terror' card pushed by the Home Minister Sushilkumar Shinde almost in a mannerism better known as 'foot-in-mouth' disease of the Congressmen.

None has miss the point that within hours of Shinde's jibe that he had reports that the BJP and RSS 'conduct' terror training camps, Pakistan-based terror leader Hafiz Saeed said, "...the world should take notice (of Shinde's comments) and declare India a state that is supporting terror on its soil after its Home Minister candidly confesses." Even a known RSS and BJP detractor, Kuldip Nayar says Shinde's timing was wrong at a time "when there is fallout in India on what is happening at the border."

On another plane, in the run up to the assembly elections, travel across Saurashtra and key political segments including Godhra and importantly Muslim pockets in and around Ahmedabad revealed that Muslims were no longer talking about 2002. They wanted to move ahead.

Nevertheless, Modi detractors had campaigned that there was hardly any effective development and Modi has only created a 'smokescreen' about it. But the turnout of historical 71.30 per cent of electorate and the BJP vote share revolving around 48 per cent—a clear difference of about 8 per cent with Congress—only proved that no one was impressed by the campaign against him.

In politically crucial Saurashtra and Kutch, which accounted for 58 seats in 2007, BJP had won 43. This time in 2012, braving the onslaught of local bigwig Keshubhai Patel's Gujarat Parivartan Party, BJP managed to get just 35 seats.

Now, a closer look at why his opponents failed.

The Congress was confused—how to deal with Modi's popularity. Once bitten twice shy after the *maut ka saudagar* (merchant of death) comment from Sonia Gandhi had backfired in 2007, this time Congress adopted a low-profile approach to take on Modi.

Arun Jaitley was right when he told journalists informally in Ahmedabad that the Congress campaign policy of not attacking Modi will fail.

In fact, Sonia Gandhi's outfit had shifted its criticism to Modi's politics of development, struggling to find attractive ways to strike at his support base. "The biggest gift for Modi (during the poll campaign) came from the most unlikely quarters—Congress. The grand old party lost the plot after initial gains in July and August with its 'Ghar-nu-ghar' scheme," wrote political commentator Shyam Parekh in his blog for the newspaper DNA.

There were folly in Congress campaign methodology and

substance too. When Rahul Gandhi told voters in Gujarat that only one man's wishes prevail in Gujarat—that is Modi—apparently many in the crowd as much in BJP camp were confused as to what the Congress crown-prince was trying to say.

Though Congress is yet to digest the 'defeat' in Gujarat, it's a fact the stain of anti-Muslim violence in 2002 is unlikely to be any obstacle to Narendra Modi's ambitions. It only made people sound almost arrogant and jocular when an otherwise reasonable man, P. Chidambaram claimed Gujarat results was actually a case of 'win' for Congress.

This takes one to a Congress foot-soldier in Bhavnagar. "Our leaders only confined themselves to Modi bashing in Delhi and Ahmedabad on television. We were banking a lot on how much damage GPP will do to BJP," lamented 30-year-old Congress worker Pankaj Thakore. GPP just managed 4 per cent and 2 seats.

Post the results, so much heckled has been the Congress leadership that all indications are that the same party who played down 2002 riots during the campaign would now play up the post-Godhra carnage yet again—ostensibly to garner Muslim votes.

But it is a different story altogether that visit to riot-ravaged Godhra during election campaign revealed that Muslims want to move ahead forgetting the nightmares of 2002 far-behind. "Post-2002 mayhem, Muslim parents want to educate their children so that they can face unforeseen crises," Mohammad Sirajuddin, a teacher in a local Madrasa had told *Power Politics*. Muslims have prospered and the crime rate among Muslims had also declined.

Another key factor that actually kept Modi on the winning side was the relentless disunity within Congress rank and file. "It's a case of losing the battle before it started. Our problem is leaders are confining themselves to Modi bashing in Delhi and Ahmedabad on television. We seem to bank chiefly on how much damage GPP will do to BJP," lamented Congress party worker Pankaj Rathore in Bhavnagar.

According to the chief protagonist Modi himself, "These elections are a victory of the people of Gujarat." In his missive after the poll results, Modi said, "For those youngsters who aspire to serve society and work towards nation-building, there is a lot to learn from the Gujarat Elections. Very often youngsters are disappointed on whether doors will open for them in a system where pedigree seems to matter more than hard work. Gujarat has shattered this cliché and demonstrated to the world that if you have the urge to serve our motherland and the ability to overcome any obstruction come what may, then you will be given that opportunity to work irrespective of what dynasty or community you belong to!"

We have dealt with Modi's electoral card in the past. On the eve of elections in 2012, Narendra Modi tried to play 'Santa Claus' to his 6 crore Gujarati voters announcing a series of bonanzas and sweeping promises with focus on 50 lakh homes for the poor, loans for farmers, infrastructure and irrigation facilities in tribal areas.

Released in the form of a 'Sankalp Patra' (commitment letter), Modi's manifesto included announcement to define and identify 'neo middle class' and chart out welfare schemes for them.

"A high-level committee of experts will be set up to identify neo-middle class. Gujarat has seen an overwhelming increase in neo-middle class due to immense multi-pronged progress and prosperity during last 11 years of BJP rule," Modi made the pledge on December 3, 2012.

The effort to focus on this section was seen as a poll-specific strategy as the emergence of this section also had increased the number of 'fence sitters' (also neo-voters) among the electorate who would not be guided simply by the traditional 'Hindutva card' as they used to during earlier polls in 2002 and 2007.

"Due to development in Gujarat in the last ten years, there has been substantial rise in this neo-middle class. We want to address their issues," Modi told the media press conference.

Echoing him, Modi's trusted lieutenant Saurabh Patel said, "The expectations of people have grown up frighteningly. We are in power for last few years. So this neo-middle class needs to be catered to as a special case." The Gujarat BJP also promised an ambitious plan of Rs. 3 lakh crore over next five years and pledged among other things to make Gujarat a Global Auto hub and Logistics Gateway of India.

"Normally people use the word manifesto, I have chosen the word 'Sankalp Patra' which means my commitment towards Gujarat," Modi said sharing dais with central leader Arun Jaitley and state leaders including Saurabh Patel.

Highlighting the housing projects, which Congress had alleged as a ploy only to counter its 'Ghar Nu Ghar' scheme, Modi had said, "In the past 10 years, BJP has already constructed 22 lakh houses. In the next five years, we will construct 50 lakh houses more. Congress in its rule in 40 years since independence had just made 10 lakh houses."

Promising higher employment in the agriculture sector, Modi, whose regime has been at the receiving end of focusing on industries and neglecting agriculture, had countered, "Agriculture will produce maximum number of employment for Gujarat. In the next five years, Gujarat will once again become the textile capital of India. Cotton farmers will be the biggest beneficiary."

To woo the farming community the Chief Minister also

had promised that his Government will 'share' the interest burden of farmers' loans. He also promised greater job opportunities for more than 30 lakh youths of the state if voted back to power.

On December 20, 2012 as the results poured in talking how the state of Gujarat had turned again saffron—but on Modi's development card; one candid observation underlined emphatically by Gujarat watchers was on the role of the 'neo-middle class'.

It's this neo-middle class that has been the big differentiator, many said and waxed eloquently how the caste and community factor probably stood diluted. Even the Modi camp acknowledged this fact and reportedly Modi told BJP chief spokesperson Ravi Shankar Prasad in Delhi to tell the national media that the absence of caste factor did not work in Gujarat polity as none bothered which caste Modi, the principal vote-catcher, belonged to.

It goes without saying, master in reading people's pulse, Modi had a sound demographic basis to speak about it. The aspirations of this neo-middle class have gone up manifold essentially because there has been an increase in urbanization as well. In the chapter on development, we have discussed how both the urban and rural living conditions have improved over the decades and it's only natural that this has happened unevenly. Over the years, constant migration for better urban facilities has made Gujarat society largely urban-driven. In other words, Gujarat is becoming more urban year by year. According to state Government officials, the rural population in the state fell by about 6 per cent to 57.4 per cent in 2011 from 62.6 per cent in 2001.

Post the 2012 December polls in Gujarat, even the Congress has sought to appreciate the fact that the rise of this 'aspirational class' has thrown open fresh challenges for Sonia Gandhi's party. Sonia Gandhi's perceived honest efforts to look for introspection and candid admission about middle-class alienation in her inaugural address at the party's 'Chintan Shivir' in Jaipur must be seen in that backdrop. Sonia Gandhi emphasised the urgent need for reconnecting with the opinion-making section of the society. "India is increasingly peopled by a younger, more aspirational, more impatient and better educated generation," she said trying to sum up the problems her party faces from these sections.

The anger of the Indian middle class on corruption and more lately against the gang rape of a girl in Delhi actually reflects the same impatience of the neo-middle class. For this section, both Modi and Sonia Gandhi are right in their respective analysis that the development and infrastructure facilities are these days viewed as 'basic essentials'. Therefore, it would not be wrong to say that the electorate of development-starved Bihar had a grudge when Rahul Gandhi had told them two years ago that "money we sent for you from Delhi do not reach you." The desi Bihari question was perfect, "toh woh paisa Rahulji ka hae ka?" (does that money belongs to Rahul?)

So this neo-India is aware and Congress old style book revolving around sycophancy and playing ever emotional card of the 'dynasty's sacrifice' often fail to evoke right response from the voters. On the same plane, we must try to understand how Manmohan Singh card went in favour of Congress-led UPA in 2009—because the people thought country's original champion of liberalization is a hero of the 'middle class'. But thanks to corruption under UPA-2 in last few years, that perception has changed a lot. In the last 2-3 years, Dr. Singh's Government has been afflicted with a series of corruption charges including 2G telecom scam, Commonwealth Organising scam, Coalgate scam wherein Prime Minister's resignation was sought, the Adarsh Housing Society meant for family members of Kargil War martyrs and on privatization of Delhi airport.

The 2G spectrum scandal had resulted in cancellation of the allocation as well as resignation and jailing of the Former Telecom Minister A. Raja of regional outfit DMK. Similarly strong words have come from the Comptroller and Auditor General (CAG) on the Organizing Committee of Commonwealth Games in 2010 which was headed by a Congress MP Suresh Kalmadi, who was also jailed.

The CAG report on Adarsh Housing Society had lamented that the action of the local military authorities acting in collusion with officials of the Defence Estates Organization enabled misappropriation of prime Government land in country's commercial hub Mumbai for the 'benefit of a select few'. The scandal had resulted in resignation of the Maharashtra Chief Minister.

The auditor on its report on privatization of Delhi's spacious airport said the process was skewed in the favour of a concessionaire. It had said CAG is 'constrained to observe' that the ministry had allowed GMR company-headed Delhi International Airport Ltd (DIAL) to use prime land of 239.95 acres for commercial exploitation at a nominal fees of Rs. 31 lakh (dollar calculation?) and a paltry sum of Rs. 100 per annum.

At the same time, in a very fishy manner the ministry had allowed DIAL to levy a 'development fee' at the airport from passengers. All these have combined together to put the Government and the ruling Congress, which has been governing India for about 50 years in last six decades, on the defensive. And not without reasons.

The neo-middle class including substantial neo-voters both in Gujarat and elsewhere in the country have today solid reasons to believe that the fungus of corruption has eaten into all spheres of life in India. A series of scandals and then on the coal blocks allocation when the Prime Minister himself held the Coal portfolio has definitely nosedived the credibility of the Prime Minister, who was credited till the other day for honesty.

The Congress and the Government refrain so far has been the CAG observations about loss is only a guess and the Prime Minister himself in his statement in Parliament on 27 August asserted that the CAG report was 'disputable'. But the damage is done and therefore Sonia Gandhi is absolutely right to talk about the 'disconnect' of the Congress party with the people.

On these backgrounds actually comes the clear difference in perceptions. The neo-aspirational and well-informed class wants to attain lofty things on their own and not as some kind of favours and populist slogans and schemes of yesteryears like the 'Garibi Hatao' or even the 'Mahatma Gandhi NREGA'.

That Modi's developmental card laced with his 2002 Hindutva sprinkling had a salutary impact with urban voters again gets testified in the fact that out of 115 seats he bagged, nearly 60 came from big cities including Ahmedabad, Surat, Baroda and Rajkot. In Rajkot, the hyped hope of Keshubhai Patel's GPP simply fizzled out. Again Gautam Thakker of the People's Union for Civil Liberties rightly pointed out that the BJP's losses were essentially in rural pockets of Kheda, Banaskantha and Sabarkantha.

So phenomenal has been Modi's success as a vote catcher that his opponents are drawing satisfaction merely on the fact that BJP's seats has declined marginally from 127 seats in 2002 which got reduced to 117 in 2007 and 115 in 2012. Importantly, prior to that in 1995, BJP had won 121 seats as against 45 by Congress and in 1998 (national peak of BJP's popularity under Vajpayee), the saffron party, that went to polls projecting Keshubhai, had bagged 117 seats conceding 53 to the Congress.

In fact, similar and convincing triumph for Modi brand had come earlier in 2002 and 2007—both watershed polls too.

In 2002, dice was cast on December 12, over 9 months after the Godhra carnage which had erupted Gujarat into unprecedented communal violence. It was country's most fiercely contested and keenly watched state assembly elections. Seeing the turnout overwhelmingly 63 per cent and more—it was clear that both the communities Hindus and Muslims have walked to the polling booths with keenness perhaps not witnessed in recent past, even not during the height of post-Babri demolition communal tension.

The Indian Express did rightly report on the event saying "Gujarat kept its tryst with a communally polarised electorate (on Thursday, December 12) as Hindus and Muslims voted with a vengeance."

According to many, future of Gujarat and the secular fabric of country's polity had been put on altar.

Modi, who has been at the receiving end of all criticism following post-Godhra violence, emerged victorious after leading the saffron party to a memorable and much needed victory. This was not just a leader and probable Chief Minister romping home but it marked the mandate crowning the much-maligned man as 'Hindu Hridayasamrat'.

The Indian Express said, "the day (December 15, 2002 day of counting of votes) belonged to Narendra Modi who, riding the wave he whipped up after the Godhra attack, delivered Gujarat to the BJP and Sangh Parivar with a two-thirds majority." It was a day, Modi had the last laugh and Gujarat could be drenched saffron.

All exit and opinion polls did not predict such a landslide victory for Modi's BJP. In fact, hardly a fortnight back a popular weekly only contributed in flattering Congress ego predicting a marginal victory for Sonia Gandhi's outfit. Major poll pundits and newspapers went to the town saying that

Congress under stewardship of Shankersinh Vaghela has managed to gain ground. Senior columnist Saeed Naqvi, known for his objective observation otherwise, had only predicted a day before that "since page one stories in almost all the major newspapers are today hedging their bets, it appears that this magical 'Hindu consolidation' has not taken place."

He was absolutely wrong.

Thanks to the polarization, BJP made a hat-trick to take control of the western border state and its vote share reached a peak at 51 per cent followed by 44.8 per cent in 1998, 42.5 per cent in 1995 and 26.7 per cent in 1990.

In Saurashtra region, where polarization was said to be minimal and Patels were said to be annoyed with the saffron party for dumping Keshubhai Patel, BJP maintained its dominance bagging 37 of 52 seats. As mentioned earlier, in 2012 too, BJP managed 35 seats from the supposed Patel-region.

BJP also swept aside Congress in Rajkot district bagging 9 out of 11 seats while making significant inroads into the traditional Congress bastion of central Gujarat. It picked up 41 out of 43 seats in the region. BJP had also surged ahead in Northern region and tribal belts of Panchmahal and Dahod showing post-Godhra riots had sought to bring even tribals under the influence of Hindutva school of thought. BJP wrested the much talked about Godhra, from where it all started, with Bajrang Dal stalwart Haresh Bhatt openly declaring that it was 'Hindutva' which bagged him the seat.

The Prime Minister Atal Bihari Vajpayee endorsed the Hindutva theory when he came out to join the enthusiastic BJP supporters at his official residence, 7 RCR in the national capital. Vajpayee said that the party cadres should start working taking *prerna* (inspiration) from Gujarat.

In 2002 as well as subsequent polls in 2007 and 2012,

analysts said primary factor has been Congress's refusal to offer itself as a viable secular force. From the very beginning since the riots, Congress could hardly inspire confidence among the battered Muslims. Just when Muslims were being slaughtered and thrown out of their homes, Gujarat Congress leaders showed very little keenness to fight the alleged communalism policy tooth and nail. A lackadaisical approach had dawned on Congress leaders and they rather preferred to play safe. Appease both sections—was the Congress mantra.

"While Ahmedabad and other adjoining places were burning day in and day out, Congress leaders sat on Dharna outside Sabarmati Ashram in Ahmedabad and even gathered leaders and Chief Ministers from other states," says *Godhra – A Journey to Mayhem* (Samskriti Publication). There were also reports that deceased Congress leader Ehsan Jafri's sister Dur-e-Shahwar herself, later had complained that no one came to help her brother when his Gulbarg Society residence was attacked by angry mob on February 28, 2002.

The mismanagement of poll campaign has haunted Congress throughout the decade between 2002 and 2012.

Even after Vaghela, another former RSS Pracharak, had failed in 2002 and also later, in 2012 yet again the Congress again banked on Vaghela.

These weaknesses gave the state's most controversial Chief Minister immense advantage.

The electoral track record of Vaghela has not been very good and he had himself lost in 2009 Lok Sabha polls.

Similarly, Keshubhai Patel has only reduced his battle as a characteristically caste-based battle—something which has been always on weaker side as compared to religious polarization (Hindutva) in Gujarat.

"Keshubhai is solely banking on anti-Modi stance. People are convinced that his problem is purely personal. That will not cut ice particularly from an aging leader," commented T.M. Desai, a retired bank official in Ahmedabad days before the December 2012 assembly polls.

Keshubhai's other limitations in the eyes of 'modern Gujarat voters' was that unlike Modi, who has admirers in corporate honchos and also in countries like China, the GPP supremo was essentially only a mofussil leader.

Analytically stating politicians and political parties are more often known as strange bedfellows. In the case of Congress-Gujarat Parivartan Party (GPP) alliance – overt or covert – in 2012 – it was truly a case of sleeping with enemies. In short, GPP led by former BJP satrap Keshubhai Patel represented the anti-thesis of Congress ideologies and philosophies. GPP is not only a caste-based outfit floated by a former Hindutva champion, it also swears by the ideologies of Sangh Parivar ideologue Deen Dayal Upadhyaya. GPP leader Gordhan Zadafia, number two in his party after Keshubhai, had in fact charged the Modi regime with 'compromising' the principles of Hindutva in order to project himself as a future Prime Ministerial candidate.

Privately Congress leaders admitted that 'greater catastrophy' would unravel once GPP and Congress have to form an alternative. "That Plan B has not been worked out yet," say many leaders adding, "it will be difficult to stomach a Keshubhai-led Government with Congress supporting it." Admittedly, it's sheer anti-Modi approach that has brought both the parties together. The result of this one-point agenda was actually well exploited by Modi's poll managers.

"By agreeing for an unholy alliance with Congress, Keshubhai has only reduced his political stature. From a champion of Hindutva in BJP, Keshubhai is today a mere casteist leader and simply seen as someone trying to score personal battle," summed up Ajitbhai Thakkar, a RSS activist campaigning for BJP in Bhavnagar.

Thakkar recalled that during his chief ministership in 1999, Keshubhai had coined a path-breaking Hindutva line when he had told a tribal in Mehsana district: "I am a tribal, if you are a tribal; similarly you are a Patel if I am a Patel. Because we both are Hindus."

Keshubhai's limitations again came to the fore when he opted for a safe seat in Visavadar in Junagadh district. Of the total 2.23 lakh voters in Visavadar, 45.5 per cent belonged to Leuva Patel community.

None can dismiss 2012 electoral debacle for Keshubhai as a fluke as in 2007 too, Keshubhai camp had urged his community (Patels) to vote for 'change' and had backed the Congress. But the result, as everyone knows was a complete shock.

Even in 2002, Vaghela was presented by Congress with an enlarged image giving the impression that by giving him the command, the party has achieved half the target. The argumentative refrain was "Vaghela is the only bull dog who can take on Modi."

We are not here to suggest that Vaghela's predecessor Amarsinh Chaudhary as Gujarat Congress President or the likes of Bharatsinh Solanki would have made electoral fortunes different for Modi. In 2012 yet again the likes of Shaktisinh Gohil and Arjun Modhwadia lost.

Vaghela, though continued his tirade against BJP and VHP all throughout, in the run up to the polls he had never opened his mouth against RSS, the principal organization of the Sangh Parivar. Often asked to comment on the role of RSS in 2002 riots, Vaghela remained non-committal and merely used to say, "why you are raising an old issue." In other words, he just could not speak against RSS, not to talk about disowning it.

In 2002 again, as electioneering gained momentum, Congress also fielded a group of religious leaders led by the popular Morari Bapu to pitch in for the party. This meant in effect, Vaghela and Congress bringing in soft Hindutva or 'vanilla secularism' as described by ace media personality Shekhar Gupta.

Writing for his popular Saturday column 'National Interest' in *The Indian Express*, Shekhar Gupta cautioned Congress a day before the ballots were counted in 2002. "The Congress, on the other hand, will find that soft Hindutva is a lousy answer to the problem of the decline of the vote-catching power of the old slogan of secularism."

In 2007 Assembly Elections too Modi had made a good synthesis of development mantra along with 'no appeasement' policies towards Muslims. He almost endorsed the questionable encounter of Sohrabuddin amid much media attacks and even vilification by rivals like Sonia Gandhi, who had called him a *maut ka saudagar* (merchant of death).

It's altogether a different chapter that Modi had in fact benefited from such gross indiscriminate kind of remarks.

In the run up to the 2012 assembly polls, Modi again talked about 'inclusive growth of Gujarat and Gujaratis'. The theme of his *Sadbhavna* Fast speech in September 2011 was, "I do nothing for minorities nor anything for majority (the Hindus)." His development card is for all Gujaratis, Modi emphasized.

If newsmaker is to attain the immortality in the pages of history; among the Indian *neta* class, undoubtedly Modi would be at top. He has well by-passed the past demagogues like Vishwanath Pratap Singh, who had played the caste card or even Indira Gandhi, who had invented the art of creating vote banks in Muslims, in Tamils and perhaps also in Punjabi Hindus—only to be vilified one day—by all these sections.

But Modi's electoral success also has lot to do with his performance as an administrator. Modi knows the art of modern management pretty well. When Tata's Nano project was hounded out of West Bengal in 2008, he knew there would be probable competition among other states to accommodate Nano car factory.

On October 3, 2008 when Tata Motors announced that they would be moving out of Singur, Ratan Tata reportedly received letters of invitation from four states. But Modi sent in an SMS which simply said 'Welcome to Gujarat'.

Ratan Tata, the then Chairman of Tata Sons, later commented "Narendra Modi promised me it would take a few days. And his few days meant only 3 days wherein in common business-administration parlance in any other states could mean at least couple of months minimum." Located 60 km from Ahmedabad, 1,100-acre plot in Sanand was passed on by the Modi regime to Tata Motors.

This piece of land where the Tata Motors' manufacturing unit came up in a record 14 months, belonged to the Anand Agriculture University for over a century. In 3 days the Gujarat government acquired the land and passed it to Tatas and there were no protests or so.

Today, many other industrial houses also agree that Gujarat is most amenable to investment and industrial growth.

In the run up to the 2012 polls, the *Sadbhavna* Fast launched in September 2011 and rather taken into rural areas of Gujarat was definitely aimed towards 're-branding of Modi'. But it was not directed to turn 'secular' overnight as L.K. Advani's misadventure with 'secular-Jinnah' was a lesson for Modi too. Instead, Modi had projected his brand equity as a 'developmental model'.

Modi's determination to stay put his core constituency, the hardline Hindutva is somewhat able to make the impact as his political honesty. So much his acceptability even among non-resident Indians that in 2007 after the assembly polls, Shreyas Suresh, wrote in his blog from Chicago: "Recent

Indian political history has seen a decline of strong and honest leaders. Mr. Modi is one of the last remaining few. People might call him an authoritarian, but the need of the moment is just that. He has not only turned Gujarat into a model state with terrific development but also given the people a corruption free Government."

All these years Modi has been very tactful too. He is constantly playing as someone dealing with an uncooperative Central Government headed by Congress-led coalition. So his repeated attempts are to play the central ill-treatment meted to non-Congress states. A day is not far perhaps when he will be able to play up the role of an anchor of the anti-Congress politics.

Moreover, there is yet another interesting feature. From time to time, Modi watchers argue he has discharged his administrative role single-handedly and played political card so authoritatively that he can be easily mistaken as a 'dictator'. The perceived image of Modi has also helped as Indians in recent past have shown tendency to prefer 'strong' political leaders. This is why, a simple analogy suggests people could prefer a whimsical politician Mamata Banerjee then well-organized communists in West Bengal.

However, it ought to be stated that though Modi has come of age and created a sort of wave as it is he who seems to be driving the agenda for political discussions on television channels as well as next day's headlines; there was a time when he was considered hardly a 'mofussil' leader like his illustrious predecessor, Keshubhai Patel. But he has proved that he is everything, Keshubhai Patel has not been.

The image of strong leadership provided by Modi has in fact many takers. Endorsing the BJP's prime ministerial candidate, former IPS officer and Anna Hazare's key aide Kiran Bedi on 9 January 2014 said Narendra Modi can provide stable, accountable and inclusive government. She wrote on social networking website Twitter, "For me it is India First! Stable, Well Governed, Administered, Accountable and Inclusive. As an independent voter."

In a television interview, only a few days before, former union minister Arun Shourie discarded the oft-repeated argument in media that Modi should tender an apology for 2002 mayhem. Instead, Shourie told CNN-IBN: "Immediately people will say he (Modi) is doing it for elections. The record is yes there was a breakdown and it has never happened again in Gujarat and I would hope that he would stand on that and not go in for this apology and so on that's nonsense." In fact, Modi has himself said that he would stand by what he has been stating all these years. "This is my USP," he asserted during one media interaction in New Delhi.

Read more at:

http://economictimes.indiatimes.com/articleshow/28608305.cms?utm_source=contentofinterest&utm_medium=text&utm_campaign=cppst

4. Development: The Gujarat Model

While working on the book we tried to enlist views of cross-sections of people on why and how Narendra Modi clicks on development and economic governance fronts, the common refrain has been that in a country where governance is mostly bottled up through bureaucratic clumsiness the face of administration in Gujarat resembles the story of co-operation—and thus, the triumph.

The Chief Minister's admirers at yet another Vibrant Gujarat meet, January 2013, gave away the credit for Gujarat's monumental developmental works to Narendra Modi primarily because what his state has achieved is still difficult and near impossible in other states across India. Devoid of red-tapism, doing business essentially is a hassle-free phenomenon.

In December 2002 Assembly Elections, Modi won a landslide victory bagging 126 out of 182 seats riding a strong Hindutva wave generated by post-Godhra incidents. Then, there was no talk of development as Gujarat had rightly emerged as a laboratory for the most militant variety of right-wing Hindu nationalism in the history of independent India. Within a month since the historic victory in the heat and dust of Gujarat polity, Maharashtra BJP stalwart Gopinath Munde announced at a rally at Shivaji Park, Dadar in Mumbai in the presence of Modi that his party was eager to repeat the Gujarat formula of Hindutva in the state.

Five years later, on 23 December 2007, the BJP and Modi yet again won the state elections in Gujarat.

With BJP already out of office in Delhi since 2004, the Congress had hoped to turn the tide in Gujarat too. But the landslide victory in 2007 with Modi's party picking up 117 seats predictably sparked off the debate whether Modi won because of his charisma, because of his Hindutva image or economic development of the state since 2001. Subjected to too much criticism for 2002 mishandling of riots, in 2007 Modi just could not repeat the Hindutva card once more. Moreover, the ignominy of 2005 when the US had declined him Visa was still fresh in public memories as well as in the memory of a shrewd politician Modi.

He could not depend solely on Hindutva discourse and therefore, he shrewdly packaged Hindutva image with the development card.

Contrast to this in 2002, immediately after the results, Congress general to the Gujarat battle Shankersinh Vaghela attributed BJP's victory to 'misuse of Hindutva' even as he sought to caution the voters against Modi Government's failure in providing jobs and water. "Victory may come and victory may go. But even Hindus would need water and electricity," he had said. Thus, governance was in the air in 2007 amid the heat and dust of Gujarat politics punctuated with Hindutva elements as well as on ways and means to fight terrorism, often considered a by-word for Muslims.

Observers feel that the single most right thing in Gujarat

under Modi is that the business and industry are treated with priority. Thus, when business tycoons from Mukesh Ambani to Anand Mahindra made a beeline for the Vibrant Gujarat Summit in January 2013 and also talked highly of Modi's industry-friendly gestures as well as policies—not many were really surprised.

Take a check list of what all the corporate tycoons said about Modi at the three-day Vibrant Gujarat meet from January 11, 2013.

"Narendrabhai has the Arjuna-like clarity of vision and purpose.... Modi's skills have acted as a huge magnet for investors and entrepreneurs from India and across the world in the past decade," said Anil Ambani. He further said, "Narendrabhai Modi dreams with his eyes open, and has an open heart and mind."

He compared the Chief Minister with the state's illustrious sons—Mahatma Gandhi, Sardar Vallabhbhai Patel and Dhirubhai Ambani.

His elder brother Mukesh Ambani committed an investment of Rs. 1,00,000 crore to Gujarat and also an additional Rs. 500 crore to Pandit Deen Dayal Upadhyaya Petroleum University. "In Narendrabhai, we have a leader with a grand vision ... Gujarat has been a pioneer state in infrastructure giving it an innate advantage," said Mukesh Ambani.

Anand Mahindra of Mahindra and Mahindra group said, "Today people are talking about China model of development in Gujarat but day is not far when people will talk about Gujarat model of growth in China."

Importantly, the sustained campaign by an army of NGO activists, secular brigade, hyperactive media and partly even judicial activism, the Modi administration has able to brave through all the pervading atmosphere of negativism.

True, Modi's legion of powerful critics is a force to reckon with. But even the worst of critics have to agree that the state of Gujarat is growing faster than any other Indian state. "...10 years on (since the mayhem of 2002) whilst the controversy is still being debated, it isn't stopping business from flowing in (Gujarat)," summed up BBC in its report on the event of the completion of 10 years of the country's worst religious violence last year.

The enthusiasm was again endorsed by corporate captains including from the United States and the United Kingdom who had blacked out Gujarat post 2002 mayhem.

Ron Somers representing US India Business Council (USIBC) called Gujarat's progress 'stunning'. "Progress of Gujarat is stunning. It has set a new benchmark not only in India but across other countries in the world because Chief Minister Narendra Modi has shown that progress trumps politics. Gujarat has achieved double digit growth because of stability and sustainability," he said. UK India Business Council (UKIBC) chair Patricia Hewitt, whose country ended decade-long boycott of the state in October 2012, also appreciated Gujarat for having maintained a near double digit growth rate in the last ten years which was more than that of China.

There are many others; the Bombardier from Canada that has built a manufacturing plant in Savli to rollout compartments for Delhi Metro in what is said to be a record 18 months.

The results are also showing, say Gujarat Government officials. In 2001, the year Modi took over office, Gujarat's economy shrank by 5 per cent due to political instability as well as factors like the killer quake in Bhuj. But by 2011, the state's Gross Domestic Product shot up to an annual 11 per cent.

In yet another turning point to boost Gujarat's industrialization situation, in October 2011 the auto maker Maruti Suzuki's board meeting in New Delhi approved a new manufacturing facility in Gujarat and purchase of land in

Mehsana district. This was after Maruti's plant faced labour related problem in Haryana.

In circa 2011, Gujarat managed a turnaround and achieved 11 per cent agricultural growth, according to State Government officials despite its fast track industrial development. His opponents attribute the success to the state of Gujarat and the people of Gujarat's 'process of survival and high talent for entrepreneurship'. But the march towards progress in the field of agriculture, infrastructural facilities like drinking water, education, employment, transportation, manufacturing and tourism is certainly heartening.

"Ten years ago, Gujarat farmers' agriculture income was Rs. 14,000 crore that has risen to Rs. 80,000 crore today. The average agricultural growth rate of the country is less than 3 per cent while Gujarat's has crossed the double digit figure of nearly 11 per cent. He (the farmer) is using drip irrigation, green house, net house and sprinkler techniques to maximize profit with minimum investment. Due to soil health card, the productivity of the land has multiplied giving new directions to the agriculture sector," the Chief Minister said in an interview in October 2011.

Contrary to allegations that the Modi's hyped developmental works has neglected small and medium sectors and agriculture also, officials say Narendra Modi's administration has pursued 'strategic planning' to bring about agricultural and industrial growth parallel to each other. It also addressed social sector issues too.

Seeking to clarify that Modi's brand of development under the banner of Vibrant Gujarat, were not basically for big industries often neglecting the social sector, in 2011 at the Vibrant Gujarat summit, they say the State Government deliberately focused on the financial uplift of rural poor to make them self-sufficient through a programme called 'Mission Mangalam'.

"In 'Mission Mangalam', not only the State Government but reputed corporate houses will also make joint-efforts. The strength of Gujarat lies in its 50 per cent population comprising of women. If women are included in the path of progress then the pace of development will be faster and widespread. I am committed to adding the strength of 'Nari Shakti' as partners to development and decision-making. For this I wished to extend economic activity support to women and created 'Sakhi Mandals' throughout Gujarat. 'Mission Mangalam' is one such enterprise that helps the poorest of the poor women. Whether it is celebrating marriage or tending to sickness of her son or daughter, she need not depend on any external help. Lakhs of 'Sakhi Mandals' have been integrated with banks leaving the management of over Rs. 1,000 crore in their hands. It is our desire to take this amount to Rs. 5,000 crore. Just imagine if this huge amount is managed by poor women, how much progress they would have really achieved," the Chief Minister said in an interview circulated through his publicity newsletter.

On the Vibrant Summit neglecting the small and medium industries, the Chief Minister says such a notion is only based on 'a big misconception'. The country's 5 per cent population lives in Gujarat which has 6 per cent of the country's land mass and its GDP share is 10 per cent. In this the contribution of nearly four lakh small and medium industries from Gujarat cannot be ignored.

The country's 70 per cent salt production is in Gujarat and the state also leads in caustic soda production (90 per cent); chemicals (60 per cent); petrochemicals (50 per cent); pharma (40 per cent); and polished diamonds (80 per cent). Business in salt, pharma and chemicals is largely run by small scale entrepreneurs and is a large contributor to national growth. This has brought in multi-faceted developments. On one hand, Gujarat is an emerging global auto hub of India while on the other hand it has also become the textile and petrochemical hub.

Under Modi's stewardship and a true CEO-like approach; Gujarat organized five Vibrant Summits in the last decade and placed the state on the world map. In the summit of 2011 alone, 7,936 MoUs were signed with investment commitment of Rs. 20.83 lakh crore. This staggeringly high investment also promised to create over 52 lakh local jobs. In agro-based industries, MoUs worth Rs. 81,600 crore have been signed.

VIBRANT GUJARAT 2013

The Vibrant Gujarat 2013 Summit has been billed as an example of a visionary approach of the Government of Gujarat towards inclusive and sustainable development.

It was the sixth edition of the summit that provided enormous prospects to the state to display its strength, progressive stand, initiatives taken to improve governance and investor-friendly climate.

A brainchild of Modi, 'Vibrant Gujarat' is a flagship knowledge-cum-investment summit started in 2003. The last summit in 2011 had seen participation of 12 states, primarily BJP-ruled Madhya Pradesh, Chhattisgarh, Jharkhand and Karnataka. Significantly, Andhra Pradesh was the only Congress-ruled state that participated in the 2011 summit.

Industry and political watchers say establishing the Vibrant Gujarat brand among non-BJP ruled states, was perfectly in line with Narendra Modi's national ambitions. The saffron-party ruled Karnataka was the official partner state for the summit while Japan and Canada were partner countries wherein participants had thronged from as many as 30 countries. The State Government officials say inclusive development being the prime focus, the key areas for development identified included: Innovation, Sustainability,

Youth and Skill Development, Knowledge Sharing and Networking. These major areas were infused through more than 127 events.

CREDITABLY FOR HIS EFFORTS

Narendra Modi has been the Chief Minister of Gujarat since 2001, leading Gujarat's population to unprecedented changes in wealth, infrastructure and social development. Officials say Gujarat's reforms are internationally recognised and have won the United Nations Public Service Award for improving transparency, accountability and responsiveness.

Over the years the state has received cumulative Foreign Direct Investment (FDI) inflows across all sectors worth US $ 7.2 billion from April 2000 to April 2011. According to officials, MoUs have been signed in different sectors. In Vibrant Gujarat 2011 alone, projects in the food and agricultural sector came through included a proposed total investment of Rs. 34,851 crore.

SPECIAL INVESTMENT REGIONS (SIRS) IDENTIFIED BY THE STATE

- Delhi-Mumbai Industrial Corridor (DMIC)
- Palanpur-Sidhpur-Mehsana Industrial Area
- Ahmedabad-Dholera Investment Region
- Vadodara-Ankleshwar Industrial Area
- Bharuch-Dahej Investment Region
- Petroleum, Chemicals and Petrochemicals Investment Region (PCPIR)
- Kalgam-Maroli-Khatalwada Industrial Area
- Valsad-Umbergaon Industrial Area
- Santalpur Industrial Area
- Halol-Savli Industrial Area

- Aliya Bet
- Hazira-Pinjarat Industrial Area
- Logistic Parks

DELHI-MUMBAI INDUSTRIAL CORRIDOR (DMIC)

A high impact industrial area within 150 kms distance on both sides of the Dedicated Freight Corridor (DFC), with an investment potential of US $ 90 billion being laid down between Delhi and Mumbai.

- DFC is a new rail transportation system with high axel, multi-modal and computerised features.
- DMIC area to be developed as 'Global Manufacturing and Trading Hub' in two phases (6 nodes) – supported by world class infrastructure and enabling policy framework.
- Investment potential for Gujarat is about US $ 30 billion (1/3rd of total investment potential in DMIC).

In the last five Vibrant events, the MoUs for investments planned amounted to Rs. 39.54 lakh crore. According to the department of industries and mines, the total investment in the state (between January 1983 and June 2012) was Rs. 11.31 lakh crore. According to Centre for Monitoring Indian Economy (CMIE), the total industrial investment in Gujarat between January 2003 and January 2013 was Rs. 20.05 lakh crore. The Department of Industrial Policy and Promotion puts the total investment in the state at Rs. 9.09 lakh crore.

PORTS AND OTHER AREAS

The easy accessibility of ports is truly vital. Gujarat already has 40 ports that handle 80 per cent of India's traffic and 20 per cent of its cargo. The state is promoting at least four private ports—Mundra, Pipapav, Kandla and Dholera. To the credit of Moditva, the energy companies Royal Dutch Shell and Total have opened a major liquid natural gas terminal in Gujarat and Indian Torrent Power has built a huge plant.

Among others, Tata Motors, DuPont, General Motors, Hitachi and dozens other foreign and Indian companies have built factories, expanded operations and invested in projects in the state. "If you are an investor in India, Gujarat must be at the top of your list," rightly analyzed one business leader of an American trade group.

Another factor on why Modi's performing governance call has such laudatory impact but is actually missed amidst the hyped debate is due to the fact that the business houses including from outside hardly bother about media campaign and constant allegations on his alleged 'hate Muslim' philosophies.

In the run up to the December 2012 Assembly Elections, travel across Saurashtra and key political segments including Godhra and importantly Muslim pockets in and around Ahmedabad revealed that Muslims themselves were no longer talking about 2002. They wanted to move ahead. The marketing gurus were little perplexed that in the month-long campaign to the polls and even before that Modi, much maligned for the 2002 anti-Muslim carnage, had tried to project himself as a 'doer', a tough leader who can command, take decisions and much importantly against whom there are no corruption charges.

With these qualities in his kitty, even Muslim voters and a few Congress opponents in the state admitted that the stains of 2002 riots only looked a humble apology. His detractors' argument that Modi has only created a 'smokescreen' about developments did not carry much weight with the voters.

"Post-2002 mayhem, Muslim parents want to educate their children so that they can face unforeseen crises,"

Mohammad Sirajuddin, a teacher in a local Madrasa in Godhra had said. Muslims have prospered in the last decade and the crime rate among Muslims has also declined, he claimed.

Adequate power availability is another crucial asset. It is a power-surplus state both in coal-based thermal power and solar energy usage.

The Asian Development Bank has approved $ 100 million loan to Gujarat to build a 500 megawatt solar park.

Fortunately for Gujarat, the state is the biggest benefactor in the proposed Delhi-Mumbai Industrial Corridor as nearly 35-40 per cent of this corridor passes through Gujarat.

In the series of Vibrant Gujarat Summits it hosts, among other global partners, joined officially to promote Gujarat as an International Business Hub, are United Nations Industrial Development Organisation (UNIDO), Commonwealth Business Council (CBC) and delegates from over 100 countries. In 2011 alone, MoUs valued at over $ 450 billion were signed. His admirers say Modi has placed Gujarat's development success in reaching 13,000 village centres by globally connecting them with broadband internet through satellite technology, the largest such network in Asia.

As stated above, Modi regime has also initiated programmes to strengthen the education and health sectors, and has also reached out to enhance the role of women force in development. "We saw the dream of parallel development of agriculture and industry a decade ago. And today in 2011 it has become a reality and is a talking-point the world over. That is why I say that Gujarat dreams, Gujarat delivers," said Modi once.

"So many things work properly in Gujarat that it hardly feels like India," remarked magazine *The Economist* in its July 7, 2011 edition. The reference is to a few glaring examples of quick delivery from the state wherein industries could set-up their units and also get going. For tyre-major CEAT, it took only 24 months to get going including the normally fraught process of buying land.

When the Canadian heavy machinery company Bombardier won a contract to supply compartments to Delhi Metro in 2007, it needed a factory site. It found one in Savli, an industrial estate in Gujarat. In just 18 months, the speed with which things moved, surprised Bombardier executives, whose managing director in India, Rajeev Jyoti has called it a "world record within Bombardier." (*The Economist*)

Needless to add, in many other parts of India, the permit process might still be grinding away. In 2008, when his project was practically shooed away from West Bengal, Ratan Tata, the head of Tata Sons, found that it took just 'three days' to find a spot for a plant to build its renowned micro car, the Nano.

Among many things that investors cheer today about Gujarat are state's good roads and ports, reliable and surplus power, business-like approach of bureaucrats with less corruption and importantly the red tape kept at a distance. Therefore, Gujarat, with just 5 per cent of India's total population, accounts for 16 per cent of the country's industrial production and 22 per cent of exports.

"Modi's strong political will and business acumen of the local bureaucrats and entrepreneurs of the state have jointly shaped investment-friendly policies to unleash the potential of Gujarat," said a local businessman. Despite 2002, largely Gujarat's socio-political atmosphere remained business-friendly. Moreover, the very fact that the state outshines all others in offering uninterrupted power supply, state-wide gas grid, rich gas reserves, extensive roads and rail network, airports and seaports makes it conducive for all types of investments to thrive. In effect, the business houses including from overseas hardly bother about media campaign and constant allegations from his detractors about 2002 incidents or the continuous legal battles related to 2002 cases. The corporate honchos laud the quick delivery system and dismiss alleged inaction during 2002 riots or even 'ill-action' later like Sohrabuddin encounter episode as small 'prices' to efficient and quick delivery mechanism.

"If you want to invest in India or set-up plants quickly, Gujarat ought to figure at the top," rightly says Sushma Swaraj, Leader of the Opposition, who, however, reportedly is opposed to naming of Modi as PM-candidate.

In fact, her observation at *Sadbhavna* Fast that when business houses approach Modi for works, they pleasantly find all relevant officials lined up in his office, has many takers.

"When some business magnates enter his office, Modi is prepared with a list of 'yes' and 'nos' to the possible questions. Most concerned secretaries of related projects are already summoned," said a retired bureaucrat.

To questions asked umpteen times as to why investors should make a beeline to their state, the Gujarat Government mandarins have pretty long answers. Some relevant check-list include: Business-Friendly Regulatory Environment, Simplification of Procedures, Gujarat Investor Portal, Investor Support Software, Investment Monitoring System, Industrial Zoning and Creation of Land Bank.

If the state is today attracting these unprecedented investments and trade, the Chief Minister's *mantra* also has a contributing factor. 'Red carpet, not red tape' is what he said and has so far been able to stick to it.

Among those convinced about resurgent Gujarat, there is already excited talk about some exporters switching from China to cost-friendly India. Sanjay Lalbhai, Chairman of Arvind Mills, a textiles maker and clothing retailer based in

Ahmedabad, told *The Economist* magazine that such a move is 'imminent' in his industry.

A write-up in the website Firstpost, titled 'Two of a kind: Why China is betting on Narendra Modi' said, "they (Chinese) perhaps find in Narendra Modi a man that China can do business with. China's ambassador to India, Zhang Yan, reached out to Modi and expressed China's interest in working together to sharpen Gujarat's industrial and manufacturing edge, which has driven it to the top of the charts of Indian states ranked on industrialization."

The article, which was widely circulated as a newsletter from gujarat@gujaratindia.com also argued that "the Chinese invitation to Modi is an astute political move and sends a very strong political signal, particularly in the context of the fact that Modi was in 2005 controversially denied a visa to travel to the US for his role in the 2002 riots.... By rolling out the red carpet for Modi, in contrast to the US visa snub, Chinese officials are making a calculated investment in the future, which they know will be well received by a leader who prides himself as an embodiment of Gujarati *asmita* (self-respect)."

On November 9-10, 2011, Modi paid an official visit to China at the invitation of the Chinese ruling party.

The dividends from Modi's China visit would be obviously in trade and investment; but there was an important diplomatic message in this engagement with the Chinese leadership. If one takes a closer view, the visit came at a time when America's global influence is presumed to be on decline. On the other hand, experts are already talking about emergence of a new economic strength in the form of BRICS—comprising Brazil, Russia, India, South Africa and of course China.

The stage is moving towards BRICS—an acronym of forum of these countries—seeking to outsmart hitherto existing economic giants in the west.

The optimism is not given to arrogance but sheer confidence. New Delhi mandarins in the Ministry of External Affairs are already calling this development as the making of a 'forceful coalition' of developing countries and Indian missions are getting active to take other members into the same roadmap.

So perhaps there was a message to the establishment in Washington from Beijing. The Communist Party of China Vice-Chairman Wang Gang gave a warm reception to the delegation led by Modi at the Great Hall of People. The Chinese political leadership does not host Chief Ministers from India every other day. So the significance is well understood.

Besides showcasing Gujarat as a destination with a suitable environment to invest and work, he also explained Gujarat becoming a major tourist destination and brought out the richness of Buddhist culture in Gujarat which solicited very keen interest among Chinese leadership. He also dwelled upon the ancient Indian and Chinese ethos, relationship, friendship, cultural and business ties. Modi had said, "To give a big boost to the economic interaction, we must emphasize on cultural exchange. I am keen to start a Mandarin language school. We also have a number of Buddhist places which can be the driver of cultural exchange." Modi stated, "I have seen growing interest among Chinese companies to work in Gujarat. We wholeheartedly welcome them. My personal visit is to reinforce that process."

Chinese Minister of International Department Chen Fengxiang, hosted a welcome banquet in honour of the Chief Minister and also accepted the invitation extended by the Chief Minister to visit Gujarat and agreed for China's participation in the next Vibrant Gujarat Summit in a big way. Modi offered the opportunities for collaboration in sports as

Gujarat has set-up a sports university. Modi also had a delegation level meeting with the Mayor of Beijing Guo Jinlong. He gave a detailed status of Gujarat and its cities as well as growing urbanization, which provides excellent opportunities for cooperation and collaboration. He invited the Mayor and his key officials to visit Gujarat and its cities to explore the cooperation and collaboration in various areas.

The entrepreneurship drive of Gujaratis as well as others residing in the state has also triggered large-scale development and also migration from the villages. Historically, villages are self-contained worlds, producing wheat, maize and other agricultural products, its artisans supplied tools and implements to farmers. But over the years, constant migration and search of better urban/modernized facilities has made Gujarat society today too largely urban-driven.

It is undoubtedly becoming more urban year-by-year, both demographically and culturally.

The rural population in the state in 2011 fell to 57.4 per cent from 62.6 per cent in 2001, according to state Government sources while from 37.4 per cent in 2001, the urban population of Gujarat too has risen to over 42 per cent. Ahmedabad, the state's commercial hub and a trader's paradise, is the most populated district in the state, with 7.20 million people. This has also seen north-bound graph by an estimated 11.94 per cent from 2001, followed by Surat with 6.07 million people, up 10.07 per cent, as per Gujarat's Directorate of Census Operations.

It is true, both urban and rural living conditions have improved over the past decades but it's only natural that this has happened unevenly. There's an estimate that the housing conditions have improved relatively more than education and health—therefore Modi Government, officials say, took an unprecedented interest in bridging the gulf in these two sectors. The 'Chiranjeevi Yojana' was launched in 2007 under which women below poverty line can go to the empanelled private nursing homes for delivery and the cost for the same is borne by the State Government. The State Government officials say the scheme has come handy both for the people and the administration in bringing down infant and maternal mortality in Gujarat. This mechanism was necessitated as an estimated 3,000 women reportedly die every year in Gujarat while delivering babies. The state infant mortality rate according to 2009 data is 48 deaths per 1,000 live birth, this figure being higher than its immediate neighbour Maharashtra.

"Most of these casualties came due to delay in delivery of health services and acute shortage of qualified gynaecologists and anaesthetists. We found 'Chiranjeevi Yojana' very handy as the Government also launched number '108' for emergency ambulance service," said Jay Narayan Vyas, the former Health and Family Welfare Minister. According to official estimates, about 20,000 infants were born in emergency ambulances whose number across the state has now risen to 450. "This is a 24-hour facility and the ambulance generally arrives at 15 minutes notice," says an official.

In effect, there's a story behind the emergency ambulance service. A couple of years ago, the blockbuster film '3 Idiots' left a few health department officials in the state touched when one of the characters lament that "in this country, there's a guarantee of supplying Pizza at half an hour notice, but no such thing for ambulance." As officials spoke about the story and dropped the idea to Vyas and the Chief Minister, both readily ordered for taking necessary steps.

The State Government also took initiatives to make Gujarat a 'global healthcare destination' adding, there are tremendous opportunities to encourage health tourism to tap the vast potential. "Gujarat can expect attracting more than 2 million patients in the coming few years," he says. The

Government also claims to have achieved excellent results from initiatives like 'Bal Sakha Yojana', 'Chiranjeevi Yojana' and 'Extended Bal Sakha Yojana'.

In yet another glaring example of innovative public-private partnership to benefit marginalised tribal farmers, Deere & Company, a world leader in the field of agricultural equipments, pledged to build a new tractor facility in Gujarat in addition to its Pune factory in Maharashtra. "This will help farmers increase their chance for prosperity and improve their quality of life," said Samuel R. Allen, the Chairman and CEO of Deere & Company. The move was aimed at making more than 500 tractors available for use by local farmers and providing the farmers access to a set of 13 different implements for various operations. This public-private partnership is the first of its kind in the agriculture sector in India wherein the company would also help ensure technical skill development and enhance future employment opportunities in Gujarat by training approximately 1,000 local individuals as tractor operators.

In education and broad social indicator sectors, officials working with the Chief Minister say, the Gujarat Government faced multi-pronged and very complex problems. Despite a tremendously heartening double digit GDP growth rate, there used to be huge dropout rate of children. Young students estimated about 35 per cent of rural children have malnourished and the child sex ratio was another yardstick to raise eyebrows.

The Gujarat Labour and Employment Department has about 9 lakh names enrolled as unemployed youths. But like elsewhere in the country too, a bigger challenge than merely giving employment is to tackle the employability of youths. Officials admit that Gujarati local youths had missed out to benefit the initial euphoria of IT and BPO revolution as corporate found Gujarati youths not adequately qualified or conversant in English. This made the State Government think of starting a finishing school-type institute and also start more practical job-related courses.

The Chief Minister also took upon himself the task of visiting schools in hitherto neglected and far-flung pockets to administer tests to students to check on the quality of education being imparted. He is accompanied by a huge army of officials and volunteers. This has helped the State Government undertake a more realistic task of launching the teacher-training programme in 2007. Every summer vacation, 2-3 lakh teachers from 9,000 primary schools are put through a rigorous study schedule in 4,000 centres across the state to upgrade their skills. There is also a scheme for master trainers in Gandhinagar to interact with these teachers via satellite connection.

Gujarat Skills Development Mission was set-up in 2010 for enhancing skills of talented youths in multiple disciplines.

Another path-breaking venture undertaken by the Modi Government is save girl child initiative. In 2005, Government started the 'Beti Bachao Andolan' and now the rate stands at 960 from 816 per 1,000 live births in 2001. "We've made this a Jan Andolan (people's movement)," says Modi. The Chief Minister also leads the 'Kanya Kelavani' drive, under which state officials travel in villages to encourage parents to enrol girls into schools. According to State Government officials, the initiative has resulted in rich dividends as now there's a growth of 13 per cent in female literacy in the state. The female literacy rate in Gujarat is now 70 per cent, and this is higher than the national average of 65 per cent.

The 'Chiranjeevi Yojana' (2006) was recognised for its innovation in delivery service but a 2011 CAG report has found that the administration has missed targets. Also the number of empanelled private practitioners has fallen in some districts as clinics don't find the incentives provided by the Government profitable enough to continue with the service.

The change in Gujarat has not swept all parts of the state uniformly, yet there is no denying that almost every village has benefited by the developmental initiatives. The villages now have round the year and round the clock electricity with state having surplus power. About 30 per cent households in tribal areas have been given tap water supply during last 5 years even as in last 3 years farmers have been provided dedicated power supply.

The benefits of various schemes like 'Jyotigram Yojana' and the ones mentioned above are now leaving impact of the hard work. Check dams and subsidizing expensive drip irrigation have resulted in dividends with the state able to record a 9.7 per cent agricultural growth till 2010. The broad swath along Ahmedabad-Rajkot-Surat and Baroda are perhaps best developed parts due to obvious reasons. A Planning Commission study, supported by World Bank, has said that Gujarat offers an example of international best practice in roads management.

Authored by Clell Harral, Graham Smith and William DO Paterson, the study 'Lessons from International Experience: Road Asset Management' has found four major reforms undertaken in Gujarat that make the state exemplary. These include reduced share of administrative cost in the capital and maintenance budget from 30 per cent to 16 per cent during 2000-2007; reduced maintenance backlog by half from 10,000 km to 5,000 km; increased annual plan budget for roads from $ 26 million in 1995-96 to $ 550 million in 2010-11. The latest allocation is about 9 per cent of the state planning budget as against 4 per cent in mid-nineties.

The Gujarat Government is said to have earmarked 500 acres of land in Mehsana district for a car-making project. It is estimated that Maruti along with vendors could invest up to

Rs. 18,000 crore in Gujarat as it looks to produce around 20 lakh units in the long run. Maruti Suzuki India is looking at a phased manner of starting car production in the state. Modi had welcomed this by saying it's a New Year gift. "It is Gujarat's New Year and this is Maruti's gift to Gujarat on this occasion," tweeted Narendra Modi after Maruti's board meeting decision to enter Gujarat.

Maruti exports around 1.38 lakh cars to Europe and Africa every year. Of these over 1 lakh cars are exported from a special export unit at Mundra Port. Hitherto all Maruti cars used to be manufactured in Haryana and transported by road to Mundra Port—the transportation cost per car comes up to Rs. 25,000. With this new manufacturing facility in Mehsana area, Maruti is expected to save Rs. 185 crore in transportation costs alone. The facility is likely to generate more than 1.50 lakh jobs.

But Modi detractors say there is much of sound and fury signifying more than what is really on the ground. Thanks to his populist announcements of schemes, the rhetoric of happiness and prosperity of peasantry and labour class is louder than the reality on the ground. There is a refrain that disparity between large and middle level farmers and small landowners and landless workers has remained unchanged if not increased. Similarly, regional disparities between irrigated areas and rain-fed areas too have increased.

However, it goes without saying that apart from gradual commercialization of agriculture and changing land system, the gradual spread of urbanization and the stitching together of urban and rural areas have also transformed Gujarat. Even far-flung and remote regions in Panchmahal district and Kutch region have been affected by urban influences through migration, improved transportation, travel and trade. More particularly, the Kutch region of Bhuj has braved through the after-effects of the killer quake of 2001.

In August 2002, the then President A.P.J. Abdul Kalam made his maiden visit to Gujarat within months since he took over as the Rashtrapati. Wrapping up his two-day Gujarat visit, his first outside Delhi as the President, Dr Kalam drove down to various villages in the Kutch region, the epicentre of the quake that claimed thousands of lives. Kalam said, "I can carry from Kutch a message for the rest of the country—that of the indomitable spirit of the people."

"When I see the type of houses built by multiple agencies, I am confident that great things are possible in the state and in the country," he said while addressing a public meeting at the tri-junction of Bagala, Modsar and Mukhana villages about 40 km from Bhuj.

According to many admirers of Modi, the difference between small towns and villages has blurred. The thickening of village-kasba linkages has gained momentum. Old timers in rural villages near Rajkot in 2009, recollected that visiting cities like Rajkot and Ahmedabad were 'once in blue moon' experience that too by upper castes and rich and only landless migrant labourers even in early 2000. But now, several vehicles move around to and fro the cities daily full of college going students, a large number of them girls, village shoppers and a neo-brand of white-collared employees.

In the end probably, it would not be wrong to say that it's likely that 5 or 10 years from now the multitude of social sector schemes launched by the Modi regime in the last couple of years or facilitated by a riot-tainted regime will show results.

5. Political Management

CHALLENGES BEFORE BJP

Anil Ambani is actually not the first person to draw a parallel between Mahatma Gandhi and Narendra Modi. Long before the business tycoon spoke about the same at Vibrant Gujarat 2013, in Ahmedabad and probably other places in Gujarat the refrain often is while one train compartment incident had given Gujarat its Mohandas Karamchand Gandhi, another train compartment incident at Godhra (in 2002) has given the state its Narendra Modi. The comparison between the two sons of Gujarat is definitely paradoxical. Probably the people of Gujarat are also torn apart between ideologies and thought process as much the state is today torn apart between its past and future.

The present is, of course, Narendra Modi. The future is certainly only in the womb of time.

In this context, after the assembly elections in 2013 threw up a mandate generally in favour of BJP but Delhi going in the kitty of Aam Aadmi Party, the refrain has been can Arvind Kejriwal's outfit eclipse Modi's mission. "The challenge before the BJP is to consolidate its gains (assembly election results). Its candidates and organizational structure should inspire confidence through its credibility. With Congress getting squeezed out, the BJP is the front-runner. It has to increase its pace of activity and penetrate into every house. The 'Modi for Prime Minister' campaign has to be blended with the 'Agenda for India'. That agenda must necessarily be specific, clear and comprise of big ideas. The big ideas have an ability to eclipse a new party which has a narrow focus only on petty corruption," wrote Arun Jaitley in an article on January 10, 2014.

On his part, Modi claims Mahatma Gandhi remains a lifelong inspiration for him and many visitors to his office including those from abroad often say that they have been gifted among other things, with a copy of Gandhiji's autobiography.

Now trying to focus on BJP politics *vis-a-vis* bringing in as the Prime Ministerial candidate for the next Lok Sabha elections, it ought to be seen how the Gujarat voters see Modi as their leader—in both paradigms the Hindutva platform as well as an architect of change on developmental front. In fact, the principal challenge before BJP would be to create the same pro-Modi wave among the voters across the country. This is why Jaitley's views in the article as quoted in this chapter earlier make sense.

Among the Gujarat voters we know of those believing firmly in Hindutva ideologies who would have voted for the saffron party in any case. But there is an overwhelming section in the state—including Muslims and other minorities—who probably voted this time around that Modi has delivered much on development and that his continuance would help achieve further prosperity in the state. According to this section, despite 2002, Modi has worked hard, enhanced the primacy of private sector and put the state on a roadmap for achieving industrial excellence.

Now, the saffron party will have to transform this aura about their new found mascot in electorally key states if not across the country. In pan-India context, pro-BJP voters could be broadly divided into three categories. One, permanent BJP voters, secondly, those who think the country's development during the erstwhile Atal Bihari Vajpayee regime has been good and compared to that the Manmohan Singh Government has failed. And thirdly and importantly, the hardliner Hindu voters who would endorse Modi and his Moditva plank—a synthesis of Hindutva champion and a firm and decisive leader. For them, Modi the administrator with a tilt to deliver also for Hindus—crucially the upper castes—is by far much better than Modi—the much vilified man by the media and the secular brigade.

In addition, there is perhaps another section of voters who want quicker delivery system and that too without greasing the palm, that is without any corruption.

Let us then examine can such a scenario be possible for BJP to achieve in the national context. Importantly for BJP, notwithstanding the talk about secularism, modernity and emergence of a cosmopolitan urban India, the Hindu assertion is also a reality today. The chauvinism has come to stay and it will not be out of context that a large section of Hindus see there is good reason to be assertive and proud of their identity.

Modi's January 12, 2002 speech at Mumbai's Shivaji Park that party Cadres and BJP voters should not be apologetic about Hindutva makes lot of sense.

This retaliation does not confine to vengeance against Muslims alone. The post-Godhra carnage was carried out with an eye for an eye theory to settle the age-old score the majority community had against Muslims. This is just one part of the story. The larger reason for Hindus, mainly upper castes to feel bitter about things—the system as is better known—that in the welfare state they know that is being practised in India—the upper castes Hindus are hardly taken into account.

This is a dangerous phenomenon emerging in the country and thanks mainly to the politics of appeasement and segmented appeals pursued by the *neta* class.

Politically, however, the BJP and Modi will find it tough to replicate their Gujarat success. Contrary to the caste-less politics of Gujarat, the Hindu vote in rest of India is basically driven along caste lines. The BJP leadership is itself aware how its hyped 'India Shining' campaign fell flat in 2004. In other words, the development in politically crucial states like Uttar Pradesh and Bihar which put together send 122 MPs cannot surpass caste politics.

So what does BJP have to do? One, consolidate its vote bank. One way of doing that is to revive the original Hindutva planks—the BJP had abandoned in its pursuit for coalition politics for the National Democratic Alliance (NDA).

The original Hindu mobilization was made possible due to the Ayodhya movement and had gained momentum with each communal backlash since 1969, followed by 1985 and the post-Babri Masjid demolition in 1992. Notably, the right wing Hindu leadership also won the support of Dalits and OBCs—especially in 1996 and 1998 polls when the slogans 'Abki bari Atal Bihari' and 'Ram Mandir Banana hai' did the magic.

In 2001, the then Prime Minister Atal Bihari Vajpayee in his famous 'Musings from Kumarakom' had rightly said, "...the movement for construction of a Ram temple at Ayodhya stuck a supportive chord in more than one political party. Had it not been so, the Government of late Rajiv

Gandhi would not have taken the kind of specific steps it did to facilitate the construction of a Ram temple at Ayodhya."

But this is only the political part of the story as far as mobilization of the people *vis-a-vis* people's voting prowess went. Then came Gujarat riots of 2002 wherein the Sangh Parivar and its various socio-political wings—Vishwa Hindu Parishad (VHP), Bajrang Dal—and the BJP reportedly made use of the volcanic situation. In fact, many say a truly orchestrated game plan is on to interpret Hinduism as "one-book, one-God religion like Islam and Christianity." Vajpayee was again right when he had pointed out that "Few can deny that Ram occupies an exalted place in India's culture.... Non-Hindus too see in him an ideal King and an embodiment of great human qualities."

Thanks to the temple movement polarization that had helped the BJP win many seats in politically crucial Uttar Pradesh. But over the years and due to plethora of factors, the BJP lost its grip in Uttar Pradesh.

One reason was BJP trying to go soft on the party's core issue. Common refrain from a large section of people including temple priests had been "people of Ayodhya will never forgive the saffron party for its alleged double standards" and forgoing the temple from its priority agenda.

"Which BJP you are talking about, the pre-1992 one or the one that compromised everything for keeping NDA in power," complained Keshavram Mishra, the in-charge of Sitaram Anna Shetra, the provider of free food to the pilgrims near Ram Lalla temple.

It is on this issue, there were some merits when news surfaced in December 2012 that BJP could field Narendra Modi from Lucknow. It is altogether a different matter, Modi himself when asked on the issue simply skirted a direct reply and merely said, "Dhanyavad" (thank you). Importantly, he did not ruled out the idea outrightly.

But on its track to return to power in next Lok Sabha elections, the BJP and the Sangh Parivar strategists have to work more minutely on certain issues.

The Sangh Parivar think-tank will do well to understand that hardliner Hindutva stance has mostly struck well in the western state of Maharashtra and places adjoining it like Gujarat and parts of Madhya Pradesh and Rajasthan.

One factor, as pointed out earlier, is that the caste legion remains a strong political element in UP and other cow-belt states and also in Rajasthan.

In Gujarat the caste politics never worked very well. Nor the caste card work fetched dividends to parties like RPI neither to BSP supremo Mayawati, who makes a robust claim over upholding the legacy of Dr. B.R. Ambedkar.

For Gujarat, it is considered that the state's historic and geographic location in close proximity to Maharashtra, which witnessed initial days of Hindu fundamentalism upheaval, also have a lot to do with the polarized polity. True, organisations like RSS were founded in Maharashtra, the network immediately spread to Gujarat and adjoining places like in Madhya Pradesh with Brahmins and upper castes mainly taking up the Shakha Pramukh roles while natives Gujaratis and others generally confining themselves to trade and other occupations.

This school of thought also points out that Hindu nationalists here always looked for leadership and guidance more towards Sardar Vallabhbhai Patel, the iron-willed Home Minister—than towards Mahatma Gandhi.

Therefore, iconics like Veer Savarkar and Swami Vivekananda carry more influence. Thus, even for Narendra Modi, none other than Swami Vivekananda, the iconic Hindu monk, is a symbol of national and vote-bank political awakening. Here lies the relevance of Modi's Swami Vivekananda Yatra in the run up to the 2012 assembly polls.

The reasons for these are simple. The Hindu fundamentalists have exploited people's anguish and strong views about partition. People in Gujarat would still like to make it clear that they had accepted the country's division with much reluctance. While Pakistanis cherish the moment of creation of Pakistan, many Indians if not overwhelming of them have accepted the pernicious two-nation theory that brought about the partition. As a result the mindset that created Pakistan not only works in Pakistan, it has resulted in a 'reactionary mindset' among Hindus in India who want that the 'partition is undone'.

Therefore, an element of justification was created in Gujarat 2002 that the violence and arson were meant against Muslims. What was witnessed in Gujarat actually echoed the spirit of the RSS slogan coined way back in 1949: "Every Shakha was an ashram where Hindus were nationalized and nationalists Hinduised." It is only in continuation of this thought process that the middle class in 2002 enjoyed robbing Muslim shops in Gujarat.

So is it right to say, such Hindus do not exist in other parts of the country? But for BJP, the bigger question will be: will such Hindus vote for the saffron party. Further importantly, will that spark off a chain reaction even among Muslims?

Here, we are led towards another interesting feature of Indian polity and issues concerning vote politics. Can BJP exploit the situation well?

Even the then Home Minister P. Chidambaram admitting that illegal immigration is one major issue had got lost in the din. From Badruddin Ajmal of AIUDF, an influential political outfit in Assam, to Hyderabad MP Asaduddin Owaisi and even the likes of Ranee Narah, Congress MP from Lakhimpur in Assam and the Union Tribal Affairs Minister, the refrain has been that the violence that claimed over 70 lives and rendered lakhs homeless was a Bodo (read tribal)-Muslim conflict.

The genesis of the insane rage in Bodo-tribal pockets in Assam actually owes its origin to population arithmetic. Only a year back, in 2011, in the violence-hit Kokrajhar and neighbouring districts, the Muslim population was accounted at about 2.35 lakh. But by 2012 July-August after the bloodbath between native Bodos and mostly Bengali-speaking Muslims; Badruddin Ajmal, chief of nascent AIUDF championing the cause of minorities in Assam, said about 5 lakh Muslims are in relief camps. So, the obvious question is, "where from so much Muslim population have come so fast." No one has tried to answer that authoritatively. One reason obviously is 'appeasement of Muslims'. The northeast watchers would also tell you that it was a misnomer to term the clash of July 2012 in Bodo pockets as Hindu-Muslim conflict.

So can BJP tap potential votes here and also other tribal hubs in the northeast?

THE ROADMAP

In the first chapter, we have spoken about the 'ideological' debate within BJP and also about its intra-party differences, a point admitted by none other than L.K. Advani himself. On January 23, 2012, the day Rajnath Singh made a comeback as BJP President almost as a reluctant entrant, Advani told party workers in the televised speech that resolving the intra-party differences will remain a chief challenge for Rajnath. In fact, not long ago, the BJP satrap had diagnosed that the biggest crisis for his party would be its comparison with Congress—the 'Congress-ization' of BJP.

The rampant infighting is certainly a key similarity the saffron outfit has found itself with the Congress party.

"We should prove that BJP is a party with a difference and not a party of differences as our opponents say," Advani had said. In fact, many attribute infighting within top ranks as principal factor for party's poor show in 2009. On the eve of polls that year, BJP probably for the first time since 1989 had started for general elections on a defensive note. Making things look further gloomy, Arun Jaitley and Rajnath Singh spat continued for few days.

On ideological platform, the infighting also leads to some serious dilemma. The unceremonious exit of Nagpur man, Nitin Gadkari after the last minute high drama only exposed the weaknesses. While this had given a chance to the hardliners to project Narendra Modi as the future face; the RSS has again pushed Rajnath Singh. Thus Modi's elevation first as chairman of election campaign committee and later as PM-nominee were faced with certain amount of opposition not only from key NDA partners like Janata Dal (United) but also from within BJP. Even the likes of L.K. Advani, M.M. Joshi and Sushma Swaraj had opposed the September 13, 2013 move when he was anointed PM-nominee.

"Prior to 13th September 2013, when the BJP declared Narendra Modi as its Prime Ministerial candidate, doubts were being raised about BJP's ability to put its house in order and declare a Prime Ministerial candidate. The post-Narendra Modi declaration witnessed a huge support for Modi. The Party cadres and the support base have been hugely enthused. His personal ratings as Prime Ministerial candidate have touched a record high. The results of the assembly elections on 8th December 2013 indicated that Modi versus Rahul debate was being overstated. Both Modi and the BJP had a decisive edge," Arun Jaitley wrote.

Thus, the future of BJP's and Modi's roadmap is more dependent on several conjectures and most of them beyond its control.

The top leaders are engaged in one-upmanship against each other than anything else. Sushma Swaraj is pitted against

Arun Jaitley so much that party watchers say her rhetoric of 'mota maal' against the Manmohan Singh government in 2011 was aimed only to seek greater mileage than Jaitley, who stole the limelight by demanding Prime Minister's resignation on Coalgate. Murli Manohar Joshi and also Advani reportedly tried to stall installation of Rajnath Singh as party chief in January 2013. Yashwant Sinha by pitching himself against Gadkari's extension has now got the tag of being under the shadow of Advani. So are people like M. Venkaiah Naidu or Ananth Kumar. Thus, it was not wrong to infer that while the decision of the BJP top brass to show the door to the embattled Nitin Gadkari was an 'absolute defeat' for RSS Chief Mohan Bhagwat, who was backing the outgoing BJP chief to the hilt, Advani had scored only a partial victory or no victory. Even as for the first time since the controversy over his praise for Jinnah in 2005, Advani had a reason to smile, Advani's intent to place a man/woman of his choice at a critical juncture when Narendra Modi wants to wrest the Prime Ministerial candidature was successfully stalled by the RSS.

Rajnath Singh had his reason to admit immediately after taking over that there were 'many challenges' before him.

In 2013, under Rajnath now, BJP had to manage a difficult election in Karnataka. While it did well in three crucial states like Madhya Pradesh, Rajasthan and Chhattisgarh, it lost narrowly in Delhi though mustered 32 members in the 70-member assembly. The narrow miss in Delhi was crucial as Aam Aadmi Party, born on the crucible of anti-corruption crusade, captured power and also for the fact that BJP is out of power in Delhi for over 15 years. The infighting in Delhi BJP is also a known fact.

In eastern India, Janata Dal(U) leader Nitish Kumar walked out of the NDA over the issue of accepting Modi as a PM candidate. Former allies like Naveen Patnaik of BJD in

Odisha are yet to re-embrace the saffron fold. BJP insiders said reviving the BJD-BJP alliance will help in Odisha, where in the 2009 polls, it drew a blank. In Karnataka, after the debacle, the party has mend its ways and won over former chief minister B.S. Yeddyurappa. It also has to manage right balance between Shivraj Singh Chouhan and Modi loyalists in Madhya Pradesh. It needs to consolidate gains in Chhattisgarh and Rajasthan and need to improve its showing in UP and other northern states to make a national impact. Having lost Himachal Pradesh in December 2012, BJP is practically out of power in the entire north—except in Punjab where it is only a smaller partner to Akali Dal.

But all these only make the relevance of Narendra Modi more striking. He is seen as a strong leader and probably someone like him at the top can bring in some discipline. The Rajnath-Modi two-hour-long one-on-one meeting on January 27, 2013 in New Delhi was thus, a significant development.

This was the first meeting between Modi and Singh after exchange of pleasantries over phone. Modi had also twitted to compliment Rajnath for assuming the new charge.

Fuelling further speculation about his intent, Gujarat Chief Minister later said that he offered the party chief that "BJP's Gujarat unit should be useful in the service of the country." This was perhaps rightly interpreted as a broad hint whereby Modi, who romped home three times in a row in the western state, has put himself more openly in the crucial race.

"There was a discussion of 2014. It was quite elaborate discussion," the Gujarat Chief Minister later told reporters as he and Singh emerged from two-hour-long meeting at the BJP President's residence in New Delhi. The BJP chief also confirmed that both the leaders spoke about the next Lok Sabha elections which are considered quite crucial for BJP and more for Narendra Modi for reasons more than one.

"We also discussed the 2014 Lok Sabha elections," Singh merely said but stuck to his usual ambiguity and chose to sidestep questions about Modi being the party's Prime Ministerial nominee. "What was to be said, has been said," he retorted.

Although Modi claimed both the leaders had 'detailed discussion' on 2014 polls, cautious that he has to do much tight rope walking. The new BJP chief has made it clear that the Gujarat Chief Minister is a 'popular national leader' but hastened to add that he would not divulge his personal opinion on the matter.

"There is no doubt that Narendrabhai is a 'desh ke Lokpriya neta' (popular national leader). But no decision has been taken yet," Singh had told reporters only two days back. The clamour for 'Modi as PM' among the party's foot-soldiers increased manifold after Modi returned to power in Gujarat. Even some BJP MPs unlike the past have gone vocal in his support.

But the BJP watchers say in Rajnath Singh, probably Modi finds a 'tougher competitor' for the top slot as compared to the outgoing president Nitin Gadkari, who despite RSS backing was never considered to have a mass base. The situation is different for Rajnath Singh, who has been Chief Minister of Uttar Pradesh and is a leader of Thakur caste with sizeable votes in the politically crucial state that sends as many as 80 MPs.

But Rajnath Singh steadfastly backed Modi's candidature all along the calendar year 2013 and often at the cost of earning rebuke from party patriarch L.K. Advani.

CONGRESS PREDICAMENT ON MODITVA

On January 18, 2013, Congress President Sonia Gandhi tried to lead her party to some honest introspection at the party's

'Chintan Shivir' in Jaipur. Among other things, she referred about the middle class anguish and how 'inroads' have been made in traditional Congress strongholds. She waxed eloquently talking about the lack of proper leadership at critical levels, the corruption and the brazen show of money.

"The Congress is facing increased competition and inroads have been made into its traditional support bases," she said also adding how in some states the party is out of power for long.

"Although I believe that being in power is not the sole purpose of political activity, this does have an adverse impact on our morale and organisational ability," she had said. Here the striking illustration was Gujarat where BJP is in power from 1995.

One observation that came out of Congress camp from Jaipur was the party's inability so far to relate itself to the new 'more educated' lot especially through social networking sites and IT tools.

It goes without saying that Modi has been making optimum use of IT tools. The Gujarat Chief Minister had understood it pretty well that a website's greatest contribution is to remove the prospect of compartmentalizing an event, any propaganda or a theory. It is this so-called worldview—actually rightly influenced by his propaganda—that has fetched him dividends in terms of investors making a beeline for his state.

He has been able to make use of IT and importantly its huge reach to his advantage and image build-up. Today, more than one newsletter regarding the state are web-posted to millions of IT/email users across the globe. And I would have no hesitation that the perceptible change in people's perception about him and especially his developmental activities reach internet users—his friends and foes alike.

The Gujarat Government officials admit that Modi understood it pretty well that internet-mediated communications/newsletters/video footage can have 'transformative impact' on people's mind as more and more people are slowly getting affected by this technology. Modi is among the first group of Indian politicians making use of the technology and even social networking sites like twitter and Facebook. He has a huge following to his twitter account. Importantly, he keeps himself updated and would not miss opportunities to pass on his comments and catchy one-liners on news and events promptly.

The Gujarat watchers admit that he has also benefited by the IT and these social networking sites and newsletters. "One likes it or not, the internet has dramatically influenced his friends and foes alike. To those who view things with jaundiced eyes of a Hindu chauvinism, his twitter messages *etc.*, tell them how Hindus have been endangered. Yet again, for others, these make significant differences in changing their opinion about Modi," said a minority community public sector employee posted in Ahmedabad.

In other words, Modi's image is being rechristened or reshaped by the internet as the web technology is definitely having an increasing impact on his voters in Gujarat, Indian citizens in general and rest of the world in varied and diverse contemporary contexts.

The best eulogizing of Modi's developmental works would be summed up in the saying that in today's world, it is not merely resources that lead one to take a decision rather it is the decision that makes the resources.

According to his admirers the best gift of Modi as the Chief Executive of the state has been to lead his Government and bureaucracy to take necessary decisions quickly. According to the article run by Brookings Institution, Modi has also taken up with the Prime Minister Dr. Manmohan

Singh, asking whether the states can have their own representatives at key embassies overseas to generate funds.

Today Gujarat is developing and it is happening rather fast. Had Gujarat been a nation of its own, according to one estimate it would be 67th richest nation in the world above many European and Asian economies like China and Ukraine.

Gujarat holds many records in India for economic development:

- 20 per cent of India's Industrial Output.
- 9 per cent of India's Mineral Production.
- 22 per cent of India's exports.
- 24 per cent of India's textile production.
- 35 per cent of India's pharmaceutical products.
- 51 per cent of India's petro-chemical production.

But can that bring in votes?

THE BJP CAMP REMAINS QUITE CONFIDENT

His admirers do not hesitate to describe him as 'injured tiger'—pushed to the wall by constant vilification. The blot of 2002 had created a sort of a crisis for him. Fortunately, for Modi, he has proved his mantle. He practically had no choice but to prove his responsibility in administration and that too on development.

Were it not for Modi having to confront a full-scale war against him by the rival politicians and the secular brigade, it is unlikely that Modi would have pushed his developmental card so hard and decisively. Maybe, maybe not!

One socialist leader claiming to know Modi personally, maintained that before being elevated as the Chief Minister, Modi was a typical lower ranked BJP *neta* and was always overshadowed by the galaxy of media savvy players like

Pramod Mahajan, Sushma Swaraj and Govindacharya. "But today things have gone in Modi's favour. He might be a Muslim-baiter; but today he has brought in sustained acceleration in growth, perceptible progress against otherwise awful toll of poverty and the image of non-performing *netas,*" the socialist leader said.

Look at the results: The same Chief Minister vilified in the nation and who was denied a US visa in 2005 is wooed by corporate of all hues. He is finding himself engaged with top industrialists within the country and overseas and also there is engagement with the global economic power like China.

His admirers have reasons, therefore, to argue that when Narendra Modi has changed the rules of Indian politics to an extent as from Nitish Kumar to Mamata Banerjee—everybody is following his footsteps by organizing business summits, why won't he fetch votes.

BJP's Rajya Sabha MP Tarun Vijay has already compared him with towering personality of Atal Bihari Vajpayee.

From what was Gujarat largely known as a Hindutva laboratory, he has now thrown in a challenge that his state should be seen as a 'development model'. His fan-following in the state is not complaining yet. Even Central Ministers under Manmohan Singh in Delhi believe that Modi's popularity is reaching new heights not because of Hindutva slogans or anything else but for his developmental works.

Modi has also set the pace for inclusive growth, something cherished and given a lip-service in most cases. There is no denying that at the national level too, despite having someone like Manmohan Singh at the helm; too much of growth has been concentrated in a narrow part of the economy—IT, BPO and some urban-based sectors. Sonia Gandhi in her Jaipur 'Chintan Shivir' speech herself admitted that providing 1 crore jobs has not been possible under the two stints of the Congress-led UPA.

But in Modi's Gujarat, there have been actions on the ground for generating mass employment with focused approach for expansion in manufacturing. The Gujarat Government, despite its lapses, has also taken steps for high-value agriculture and food processing.

Therefore, what can be the measure of Modi's success rate on the developmental front? He has put the subject of rebalancing the growth chart on the agenda. The question in Gujarat and in those minds interested in Gujarat affairs is: Whether his developmental saga has to be checked or reversed? On the contrary, the clamour is for taking these to the newer heights, as a key minister in the Modi cabinet summed up.

When it comes to analyzing the success tales of Modi in the last decade, perhaps it is only natural to try to understand how the Chief Minister's popularity has grown.

In all realms of governance and socio-political epitaph today, Gujarat's story is the story of Narendra Modi. It is a replica of Jayalalithaa culture and a unique synthesis of the same style one had in Andhra Pradesh under Chandrababu Naidu or Jyoti Basu in Bengal.

Like the Leftists, BJP too is a cadre-based party but it is not the party machinery but what matters significantly is what the Chief Minister is saying or doing. True, these are nothing new, but yet there are a few stark exceptions too.

UNSTOPPABLE JOURNEY TO THE PMO

Thus, in the end, we have reasons to argue that one day Narendra Modi will address from the ramparts of the Red Fort. And that day would come sooner than later. Modi's conflicting images have so far made things interesting as well as curious. But it ought to be stated that his Hindutva zealot image is working as a RSS favourite—despite certain reports and presumptions of differences.

By the end of January 2013, the BJP and the Sangh fountainhead RSS sought to move ahead in giving Modi bigger role for 2014 polls.

Notwithstanding hiccups including certain reservations from Shiv Sena, the Gujarat Chief Minister remains unstoppable politically and in modest term, a 'national leader' as his party colleagues say. In the words of new BJP President Rajnath Singh, "there is no doubt that Narendrabhai is a desh ke lokpriya neta" (popular national leader).

Though Sushma Swaraj has expressed reservation indirectly later, in the run up to the December 2012 polls, even Sushma had endorsed Modi as PM material.

The Leader of the Opposition in the Lok Sabha had said at Vadodara on December 1, 2012, "As far as the Prime Minister's post is concerned, there is no queue but there are no two views about it that Narendra Modi is a competent candidate for the post."

The media interpretation was that Modi's chances of being chosen as the BJP's Prime Ministerial candidate for the 2014 general elections had brightened. Swaraj had never spoken openly about the possibility of Modi for the top slot, let alone endorse his candidature. In fact, her previous refrain used to be: "Modi's magic and charisma have worked in Gujarat but it is not necessary that everybody's magic works at every place."

Her statement had come a week after her counterpart in the Rajya Sabha, Arun Jaitley, had said, "since so many leaders have campaigned in Gujarat, it indicates that the entire BJP is behind Modi. We are here to give our party a historic victory." In September 2011, after the Supreme Court had given a sort of reprieve to the Gujarat Chief Minister on the riots case of 2002, Sushma had hailed the ruling saying Modi has sailed through the 'Agnipariksha'.

Actually, in more ways than one BJP finds him unstoppable. And there are good reasons and credit ought to be given to him. Despite a full-scale war against him on the 2002 mayhem, Modi's characteristic way of handling it by answering his foes through development had brought him immense dividends. He has proved that it is always wise to move ahead and even a prominent Christian leader said in Ahmedabad that it's however true that post-2002 the conditions of Muslims have improved a lot. Importantly, there is also drop in the crime rate among Muslims in their pockets, Jamalpur area in Ahmedabad and also hubs like Godhra. So the hostile whispering against him in the party has made way for such endorsements.

Until recently, the stance by analysts has been that till his name is cleared off all charges for the 2002 riots and other high-profile cases like Ehsan Jafri, Ishrat Jahan, Sohrabuddin and Sanjiv Bhatt and several others, it would be extremely difficult for Modi to find himself acceptable to pan-India voters. But the dynamics of politics is actually in the hands of the people. And the people of Gujarat have demonstrated their support for him. A section of BJP voters and probable BJP voters—the neo-middle class as has been discussed elsewhere in this book—would come to vote only if they see Modi on the horizon. The peak of BJP's popularity in 1990s, none should forget, also coincided with the peak of popularity of Atal Bihari Vajpayee.

Modi has attained that popularity level—something his detractors know but would not admit. This is why BJP found it impossible to ignore Modi. Thus, even RSS backed naming him the PM-nominee. In fact, his popularity can be understood from the fact that on October 27, 2013, in Patna people braved through bomb explosions just to listen him. In other places also, his speech and public appearance had great acceptability including in southern states.

In fact, the Patna rally was also a pointer that Narendra Modi is no longer just the man with political momentum. By his calm composed behaviour at the rally where 10 lakhs braved bombs just to listen him, BJP's Prime Ministerial candidate had perhaps overshadowed Atal Bihari Vajpayee's popularity. Thus, there is so far no stopping of Namo juggernaut.

Many of his admirers went viral on social networking sites that day, as a true statesman Modi neither panicked nor displayed anger. Rather at the fag end of his speech, he exhorted the large gathering, a record turnout of nearly 10 lakhs, to go home peacefully and in calm.

"Aap log yahan se jab jayenge, shanti se apne gaon jaeyenge ... koi accident nahi hona chahiye" (when you all walkout from this venue, please return home in good health and peace, there should not be any mishap), these words from BJP's PM-nominee almost brought tears in the eyes of few other BJP leaders who knew about the terror strikes targeting Modi.

With the kind of security preparedness as if jungle-raj or rather the 'Indian Mujahideen'-raj had taken over the state capital, mere announcement of cancelling of the rally would have put the streets in chaos and large scale devastation was inevitable.

In contrast, the less said about the role of the state government and the police under Nitish Kumar, who till the other day tried to offer himself in the political citadel as an administrative messiah.

"Clearly, Bihar Chief Minister Nitish Kumar had done his best to throw Modi to the beasts.... However, the beasts contended themselves setting off low intensity blasts," wrote blogger Manish Anand, a journalist.

The modern Indians do not want to live with the past and thus the stress is on governance. He has proved that he can deliver and he does not have to say this. The corporate honchos and even the western countries will oblige him.

The unpopularity BJP attained for itself in Karnataka due to corruption is a glaring example. So has been the question of BJP leaders in other states and also in the centre from 1998-2004. Even people talk about party patriarch L.K. Advani that as Home Minister he was behaving more as a 'balancer' and often did things as a Congress Home Minister would have done. These stigmas do not stick to Modi, a person known as a performer and more importantly who stands by what he says.

Modi's steadfast denial of saying sorry for 2002 mayhem is a point in case.

There's no doubt, Gujarat has achieved multi-pronged development under Modi. The Gujaratis have rewarded the Chief Minister Modi thrice in a row.

By his victory in 2012 polls, Modi has proved the prophets of doom wrong; something Chandrababu Naidu could not in Andhra Pradesh. Today, Gujarat is being compared with the manufacturing hub of China. Ace journalist Kuldip Nayar wrote in September 2011 that the BJP tried to project Modi on the national scene by his *Sadbhavna* Fast in September 2011, the saffron party did not attempt in any way to wash away the 'bloodstains of Modi's administration'. He further says, "The development work goes to his (Modi's) credit. But the Gujaratis are a gritty, hardworking community and will do in every clime," he wrote in his column 'Between the lines'. (September 22, 2011, *The Statesman*)

In the ultimate, it goes without saying that Modi's development card coupled with a characteristic mix of Hindutva and parochial Gujarati pride has changed the rules of politics, much as some of his bitter critics would wish to deny.

One long-term impact is that Modi has been able to create a legitimacy for himself in states like Tamil Nadu and Punjab as well in overseas countries including China. Along with brand Modi, there is also talk about brand Gujarat as an industrial hub. This is a great success and one that is being followed or aped in several other states. On November 24, 2011 addressing an interactive session with industrial captains and diplomatic gathering on the theme of 'Bengal Rising: Land of Opportunities' in New Delhi, Mamata Banerjee announced launching of a business summit in January 2012 in Kolkata, the immediate comparison was with Modi's Vibrant Gujarat. This is certainly a true measure of Modi's achievement braving against the odds one does not know any Indian politician has faced since country's independence.

The key question, therefore we have tried to hurl up is not whether Modi's developmental works have succeeded or not; but how far these were able to give him a new image.

And the answer to this is rather mixed. Narendra Modi has emerged as a catalyst of change—a transformation where in politics also means moving ahead and governance means delivery and not merely segmented appeal or appeasement. Modi is undoubtedly a Hindutva icon, who stood by Hindus during the mayhem and who is not apologetic about the Hindutva. He is also a development man. But in short, it is not wrong to call him a man ahead of his time.

The history of last decade in Gujarat is the story of Narendra Modi. This period was not only a time of political and economic changes, it has been a time of new socio-political identity for the commoners both in his state and outside. A modern secular Indian youth—either Hindu or a Muslim—hates the perception of appeasement and quota raj.

As a small town man and that also from a smaller caste group—Ghanchi—Modi has proved that what ultimately matters is what you do and how you perform.

What does it matter to be an upper caste Hindu today? The protagonists of politics of segmented appeal do not have an answer for these.

Therefore, the vocal television anchor Arnab Goswami had a point, many thought, when he asked how could the caste of A. Raja be a factor when someone had to talk about the corruption in 2G scam.

But having said these, we know, the real challenge in governance in Gujarat has been and still continues to be the challenge to ensure enhanced social security and communal harmony. But it goes without saying that the concept of 'social security' is not a straightjacket phenomenon as it might appear on the face value. The scale of communal problem by which an ordinary Gujarati, either Muslim or a Hindu, is threatened actually cannot be appreciated in a city like Mumbai or many other parts of the country. Here the rate of communal tensions always ranked higher. The primary question, security for whom and from whom/what would be very interesting to answer. In Gujarat, both Hindus and the Muslims have been oppressors.

The communalism menace rests actually on the menace of absence of social leadership.

Gujarat's major problem truly has been its breakdown of social structures. There is absence of social leadership and unlike the past, the state has been unable to put up strong leaders. See for instance, Mahatma Gandhi, Sardar Vallabhbhai Patel and even Mohammed Ali Jinnah were from Gujarat and in later stage; it gave Morarji Desai and others. Can anyone contest that even states like Bihar or West Bengal have faced these problems?

But in Gujarat, today, the scene is different. The Congress

is dreaming to oust Modi by merely playing soft Hindutva card and depending on a former BJP and RSS turncoat, Shankersinh Vaghela. The Congress did not hesitate to work on a latent tie-up with Keshubhai Patel, a mofussil variety and also considered a more strong votary of Hindutva.

Social security and harmony signifies a complex process which embraces key components like Hindu-Muslim relation, Gujarati non-Gujarati relation, effective policing, speedy and fair judicial system, role of other social organs. On these Modi's detractors have little to complain although often a hyped debate is hurled over his comments on malnutrition. Ultimately, the debate comes down to one point—If he can bring in votes and ultimately seats in the lower House of Indian Parliament, Modi will make it.

6. Why India will Vote for Modi?

In one of the previous chapters we have dealt at length on what makes Narendra Modi click from 'popularity' point of view. In the passages below we would like to examine why in the next elections, people of India could favour Modi and how.

Before going into details, one needs to address what are the issues in the mind of the Indian voters as they approach the next round of parliamentary elections. Well, a section of secular brigade including self-employed crusaders of secularism in media would harp on 2002 riots and try to rake up the issue of minority insecurity. None other than the country's Home Minister Sushilkumar Shinde is trying that and in that attempt has brazenly spoken about states to go slow on criminal and terror related cases against minorities.

BJP's former and 17-year-old ally, the Janata Dal (United) or JD(U) and its leader Nitish Kumar did it much eloquently.

This 'secularism' card has been played even by the Congress though in December 2012 assembly elections in

Gujarat, Congress had decided to stay away from raising the 2002 holocaust.

Notwithstanding this double standard, on the other hand a large section of Indians are more concerned about more crucial issues like corruption, growing prices of essential commodities, general failure on law and order front, terrorism, failure to handle repeated insults from Pakistan, effective developmental works, adequate power supply etc.

For common man in the country, Hindus as well as Muslims and other minorities, the issue is more about bread and butter and economic stability.

The absence of good governance, security to life and property and 'honour', especially for women, bothers Indian voters most.

Unfortunately, the economic prosperity and a semblance of stability people had experienced at the start of the new century has given way to economic recession—both global and at national level. This has brought in a pervasive depression and thus, it is not without good reason that Modi says no Government since independence has earned so much 'hatred' than the UPA regime. Thus, a vote for change—that is anti-establishment is only on expected lines. Now, how much that anti-Congress vote would travel to BJP-led NDA or Narendra Modi's kitty remains to be seen.

In a country where governance and development are mostly bottled up through bureaucratic clumsiness and infrastructure hurdles, the face of administration under Narendra Modi to investors—small and big ones—resembles the story of cooperation and triumph.

In terms of looking for answers on what really makes Modi click on economic front; one can firmly say that the single most right thing in Gujarat under Modi is that the business and industry are treated with priority.

The 'performer' factor in terms of governance, the BJP foot-soldiers from Baroda to Bengal believe, is actually a catch-point to encash against the leadership of Dr. Manmohan Singh or Rahul Gandhi at the national level. Modi's image, they say in the ultimate is pro-development and also pro-urbane and youth-oriented—a certain contrast with a 'weak' Manmohan Singh or even untested Rahul Gandhi. Modi's successful use of Information Technology and his net savvy approaches with enhanced involvement on social networking sites has actually gone in his favour immensely. Not so curiously, Arun Shourie argues that Dr. Manmohan Singh's presence on the political horizon is the greatest asset for Modi.

Significantly, while the likes of Manish Tewari, vocal Congress spokesman and Information Minister, had sought to advise the corporate captains to stay away from Modi because of his 'Hitler-like' functioning styles, the Congress leadership in their 'Chintan Shivir' in Jaipur have actually sought to learn a bit perhaps from Modi's page by talking about emerging neo-middle class and also on the importance of social networking sites. People of India are also anguished about the rhetoric of Congress leaders like Tewari as one Ahmedabad based businessman said angrily, "every time Manish Tewari or Digvijaya Singh open mouths, Congress lose out a few thousands of votes."

In December 2012 Gujarat elections, Modi's manifesto precisely dealt about neo-middle class.

Now, let us see Modi's appeal to various sections of Indian voters. On April 8, 2013, Modi interacted with FICCI Ladies Organisation in the national capital.

That he is 'single' for whatever reasons did not come in the way for Narendra Modi to successfully reach out to women of India, especially women Inc through the platform of FICCI's Ladies Organisation (FLO) as he fully exploited the opportunity to project his views on 'women empowerment' and the Gujarat model of development for the country.

Coming a few days after Congress Vice-President Rahul Gandhi's encounter with corporate India at the annual meeting of CII, comparison between the old war horse Modi and the untested Gandhi scion was inevitable.

While Gandhi spoke of tiresome generalities, Modi focused on empowerment of women. Modi came out as a master of powerful articulation and someone as an insider in the administration apparatus—as a Chief Minister—who knew about the problems unlike Rahul who preferred to speak as an outsider talking throwing in metaphors like 'beehive' but hardly offering any solution.

At the end of the session, many said it was yet another case of Modi came, saw and conquered.

Speaking on the theme, 'Unleashing the Entrepreneurship Within', Modi used the simple examples of Lijjat Papad, Induben Khakra and Jassu Ben's Pizza to illustrate how the women of Gujarat had shown they were no strangers to entrepreneurial skills. And how the women in other parts of India could also exploit their own talent.

The message was clear: Modi was willing to support them (women) given a due position and authority to do so.

On the same day, he addressed another session Think India Forum, wherein he spoke at length on various issues of governance. In fact, Modi made optimum use of the platform to unleash his personal manifesto for the country too.

Though sounded quite ambitious, many in the audience were left mesmerized by the promising rhetoric of the Chief Minister of Gujarat.

Think India Forum is a brainchild of Raghav Bahl, founder and Managing Director of the Network18 media group that includes CNN-IBN, CNBC-TV18 and other TV properties and several digital publications, including Firstpost and Moneycontrol.com.

Widely seen as the party's prime ministerial candidate, Modi did talk about economic reforms, supported the policy of privatisation and backed FDI in various sectors, but discarded it for retail in tune with his party line.

"The system of governance is losing credibility, which poses a grave danger. The big danger is when there is lack of trust in governance. People look for other avenues for justice and it leads to social deterioration," he said. These views were endorsed in circa 2014 by Congress strategist and Rural Development Minister Jairam Ramesh. Calling that AAP is a 'wake up call' for established political parties, he said if these parties did not pull up sleeves and change the nature of game, AAP like 'protest movement' would mushroom in many cities and towns across the country.

On his part Modi also elaborating on his model of governance in Gujarat maintained that the divide between the Centre and states was hampering the country's progress and underlined the need for bridging it.

"Good governance means to win the trust of the people and tell the people what you are doing and why you are doing and involve people if possible.... That transparency is lacking," he said.

In other words, he was telling the kind of differences his party and a possible Government under him would try to achieve. In fact, this way he was telling the voters why should they vote for his party and him.

He had also mooted a P4 model of including people in various initiatives of the Government with the private sector. "We have to go one step ahead of the PPP model to a P4 model of people-public-private-partnership. We have to inform people what we are doing, involve them and then see how we can work wonders," Modi said.

In a suggestion, which could generate controversy and probably also difficult to implement, the Gujarat Chief Minister mooted that the Ministry of External Affairs, country's foreign policy engine room, be split into two, one catering to South Asian neighbouring countries and the rest at the global level.

Modi's take was that different approaches were required to cater to neighbouring countries where there is lot of muscle-flexing and problems are complex; on the other hand at the global level India could pursue the agenda of international peace, he suggested.

Even in the past, the Chief Minister had suggested to the centre to allow states to set-up cells in foreign missions wherein concerned state representatives could lobby with global industrial captains to garner investment in the states.

He also suggested for improvement in governance and lamented why it was mostly entangled in files. "All governance in India talk about outlay, not outcome ... governance is more about outcome, results," he said.

Likewise, he said education should be made job-focused.

Commenting on the way in which politics affects decision-making power of the Governments, he said that priority for political parties and leaders in India was to win elections and remain in power.

"All decisions are taken keeping an eye on the next election. Political parties are under pressure to avoid or delay decisions dues to elections."

These were certainly part of a broad 'Modi manifesto' on governance.

APPEAL FOR GENERATION NEXT

Now let us look at his appeal to the younger generation. On February 6, 2013, Modi almost played a Management Guru to students of capital's premier Shri Ram College of Commerce. In fact, within hours after Narendra Modi made his venture with lung power—albeit a successful one—one Minhaz Merchant twitted eloquently: Modi's P2G2—pro-people, good governance, Congress's P2G2—poor people, give goodies.

The story is well-narrated indeed. In his speech at an indoor stadium, Modi spoke about his definition of government's responsibilities saying, "the foundation of emphasis about governance is P2G2—pro-people, good governance." Eyeing a broader platform nationwide, the Gujarat Chief Minister played his 'Gujarat Model' developmental card to the hilt and packaged it with a clarion call to focus on the need to tap the potentials of the youth force in the country. Delivering a lecture on 'Emerging Business Models in the Global Scenario', Modi made optimum use of the occasion to package himself as a developmental messiah especially to the educated younger generation.

And what was the result? The takeaway from Narendra Modi's path-breaking address to commerce students, a large number of them girls and have little to do with Modi's brand of politics, was that the most vilified Indian politician has set the dream going among youngsters for a Vibrant India.

Modi struck chord well with the youngsters with his message to 'rebrand India' as he used college canteen one-liners and phrases like, 'google guru', 'chips in a teacher's mind' and 'The Government has no business to do business'.

Importantly, students were not bored even for a minute which also shows the prowess of his gift of the gab. He in the process surpassed many masters of oration—the likes of Atal Bihari Vajpayee and George Fernandes during their heydays.

The usual epidemic of scepticism, those who attended the lecture said, was missing for a change.

"Not just I, everyone around me was listening with rapt attention to him. When he asked us for time to speak a little longer, the whole auditorium literally screamed 'yes'," Radhika Gulati was later quoted in the media. Now whether Radhikas really come out to vote or stay away from the booths on polling day could be debated some other time.

"Meri soch alag hae" (I think differently), Modi had told the students seeking to project himself 'different' from run of the mill political class.

He asserted that while others especially younger ones seem to be thinking of running away from the country to make careers, he has the confidence and also the experience of delivering under the same circumstances of Government functioning.

"Everyone thinks they want to run away.... This is my fourth term as the Chief Minister of Gujarat, and from experience I know that even with the present set-up, same constitution, same rules and regulations and same bureaucracy, we can make progress and achieve much more," he said.

Modi used several examples of how his Government has generated development and growth.

Prior to that as he walked in, the students screamed and gave him a loud applause generally given to cine stars. He appeared a virtual role model, a symbol—they were waiting to listen.

They were not disappointed. Modi detractors could not find much fault-line in his speech too as Modi stayed away from politics, did not name his favourite punching bags—Sonia or Rahul.

In other words, it was truly the re-emergence of a 'Vibrant India under Narendra Modi' and about whom—even the European Union has now ended the boycott.

Holding a glass of water, an image that lasted for days on

social networking sites, newspapers and magazines, Modi had said "while someone would describe it 'half-empty' and other the 'half-full', I see it as a 'full glass'—with water and air."

The catalysts for the success of his state and that way also of his—to continue the developmental spree in Gujarat, he pointed out were 'self-belief and optimism'.

"I am a very positive man, I believe we can change the situation," he said adding such a pledge by the younger generation too has become relevant in the wake of Swami Vivekananda's 150th birth anniversary being celebrated this year.

"I told a diplomat who had come to meet me recently that our greatest challenge is how to use opportunities—one of them is the youngest population we have in the world. And secondly, we have immense natural resources, especially in eastern India," the Chief Minister said.

The impact was telling from the moment the address was on. Minutes later, one Central Government official attached to a key central minister said in a Facebook chat: "I feel Congress shouldn't rule for next 15 years to pave way for economically viable and a more strong India under Modi."

One youngster was more crude in ventilating his opinion. "Time to say—jahan pana tusi great ho ... tohfa kabul karo"—he said eluding to a much popular scene from blockbuster '3 Idiots'.

So, the takeaway was Modi's emergence of at least as a man who has set the dream going among youngsters for a Vibrant India. He described youths as 'new age power' and not merely 'new age voters' as by other political class.

"The past two years have taught us that the Indian middle class can no longer be defined by mere demographics. Whether he will ever be the Prime Minister (PM) and whether his being PM is a good thing are questions that time and circumstances will answer. But Modi's performance at this premier Delhi college stamps him as the one Indian politician who truly has his finger on the pulse of a very large section of the population," wrote a senior journalist with *Live Mint*.

As students filmed Modi and his speech in their mobile handsets and later jostled among each other for autographs and photographs, many said, Modi could project himself successfully into the shoes of a reformist and someone who can deliver—thus, posing a direct competition to Manmohan Singh, country's original reformer whose test as a performing Prime Minister has failed even his admirers.

"Narendra Modi flagged his ambition to be Prime Minister, choosing 'the disciples of Google Guru' to unveil his 'vision' of a brand new India that would minimise state intervention, maximise 'good governance' and capitalise on its 'greatest asset' called the youths." (*The Telegraph*)

IMPACT OF MODITVA

However, a section of media sought to ignore the event—thanks to their reasons, editorial discretion and of course the prejudiced mindset.

"Why generally a complete newspaper, *The Hindu* gave a total miss to Narendra Modi's Shri Ram College speech will remain a journalistic puzzle, if not educated about it??"—went a Facebook message.

The Hindu's editor Siddharth Varadarajan said in twitter "We refuse to be part of the herd. Every story on our Page 1 was far more newsworthy than a speech by a CM to a Delhi college."

This is perhaps the beginning of a new polarization. The paper was dismissing Modi as 'another Chief Minister'! Of course, later it turned out more than mere academic exercise why the Editor was shown the door by the premier newspaper management allegedly for his pro-Congress slant.

But the real underlining message ought to be understood more objectively—why even VHP leader Ashok Singhal had dared to compare Modi's public acceptance with that of the illustrious Pt. Jawaharlal Nehru. This came although in the last decade, Modi, on his part has rendered VHP into the periphery of Gujarat politics. Lately RSS chief Mohan Bhagwat also backed Modi. "People know what is in your heart. The whole country is echoing with the same voice. And that is why we should not interfere in what should be done. They (BJP) will have to take a decision on what is to be done," he said in Allahabad in February 2013 after several speakers spoke in favour of projecting Modi as prime ministerial candidate.

The polarization only seems to be getting obvious as giving a new twist to the raging debate on projecting Narendra Modi as the Prime Ministerial candidate, the then NDA convenor and JD(U) president Sharad Yadav maintained that the Gujarat Chief Minister's name was being pushed by the corporate world and cautioned them from playing politics.

But all said and done; Moditva as an enigma remains clueless chiefly to Congress and the secular brigade. There is a reason to believe that jittery over Moditva Congress leadership has thus gone overboard to prove itself as 'a performing regime'. Thus, the UPA-2 wrote itself in history by hanging Ajmal Kasab and Afzal Guru in a span of little over two months.

HOW BJP LEADERSHIP BATS FOR MODI?

Actually, by March 2013, about one-and-half-months since Rajnath Singh returned to head the BJP replacing Nitin

Gadkari; enough hints have been dropped that the saffron party was too willing to push the case of their illustrious headline-hunter Narendra Modi.

In a rather curious turn of events on April 10, BJP adopted a strong line to dismiss argument that Modi is 'not a secular' leader. No less than BJP Chief Rajnath Singh himself told Arnab Goswami of 'Times Now' in an interview that Modi is a 'secular' leader and added that a "non-secular person could not survive in BJP."

Next day, the party spokesperson reiterated the stand that Modi's 'secular credentials' could not be questioned. The party spokesperson Nirmala Sitharaman told reporters during regular briefing at the party headquarter that "party stands by the statement made by party president on Modi."

These statements came at a time when JD(U) and its leader Nitish Kumar were trying to make an issue of 2002 mayhem and oppose Modi being projected as the Prime Ministerial candidate.

The BJP's official line on 'secularism' that no non-secular person can survive in the party is actually seen as a strong defence of Modi and also taunting JD(U) that "if you want to do business with us, you should be able to do it with anyone among us."

Prior to these in a series of developments, Modi had actually opened up before the national audience.

On 16th March, addressing *India Today* conclave, Modi unveiled 'India governance' plans.

"The way I am functioning is my USP.... Nothing wrong in this," he had said dismissing suggestions possibly on the 'need' for healing touch, a veiled reference to the 2002 mayhem.

"I have answered all these questions in the past," Modi made it amply clear.

He was also grilled whether he still is a 'divisive figure';

the Chief Minister said, "I cannot analyse that myself ... but in my everyday life I have never experienced that. But if there is something like this, I will take a corrective step."

Making optimum use of the occasion, Modi had virtually unveiled his 'India governance' plans and made a strong case of certain reform measures like allowing railway infrastructure to the private operators.

But he skirted a direct reply on whether he is personally interested to take up the Prime Minister's post after the next general elections, he said, "Jivan me kabhi bhi banane ke sapne na dekho, kuccha karne ke sapne dekho" (never in life dream of becoming somebody, it's important to dream about doing something).

Answering a question, he defended his phrase that Secularism means India and added, "we should work for 100 per cent of citizens.... It includes all, it answers all questions."

Modi also strongly batted for greater involvement of common people and private operators in governance and stressed on the importance of redressing the grievances. "It is not enough to make only a bus station; the effective governance should also be to ensure that the conductor in that bus station behaves properly with the people," he said. This remark was actually to challenge Congress who over the years thought just enacting laws—from NREGA to Right to Information Act will ensure its victory elections after elections.

Citing the instance of railways, he said there is need to ensure rail connectivity to all the ports as a long-term plan to change the face of development.

He also said the railway infrastructure should be let out to the private parties and mooted introduction of Pilgrimage and Tourism railways.

Taking a dig at the Congress leadership which has

brought in a number of legislative steps in the recent past, Modi said, the country needs 'action' not Legislative Acts.

Referring to UPA's NREGA scheme, he said there is a need for Development Guarantee Act and mooted that people should be motivated to contribute for the country.

"This is how Mahatma Gandhi had motivated ordinary common people to work for country's independence. He had told the artisans that your work is working for the nation," Modi said.

Modi also advocated for cordial Indo-Pak relations along with sound relations with other countries in the South Asia but said the same policy must ensure 'country's interests'.

Defending the BJP decision of opposing FDI in retail, he said the party has opposed it because allowing FDI in such high scale would reduce India to a dumping ground.

We deal with the same question raised earlier, why would India actually vote for Modi. Well, many believe Modi does represent an idea that appeals to voters.

Talking about objections to Modi's claim to the big post by Nitish Kumar, long-time BJP watcher Swapan Dasgupta wrote in a blog piece, "If Modi does represent an idea that appeals to voters at a time of national drift, Nitish needs to pause and re-think. He must consider the consequences of opposing a campaign based on fulfilling India's potential through rapid development with a sectarian question mark.... As a seasoned politician, Nitish should be wary of being led by people who aren't adept at deciphering the writing on the wall."

GOOD MARKETING STRATEGY

Without doubt politics these days is also about pushing the agenda well, the marketing as is generally said.

As we have discussed partly earlier who can dispute that

'Brand Modi' is essentially about exploiting the IT tools to communicate his message effectively.

"When Rahul Gandhi spoke of abysmal number of days that the Gujarat assembly met for, Modi tweeted within hours, asking him about the number of hours he had spent in Parliament as an MP! The idea to market Modi is clearly to make his presence so pervasive that it becomes difficult to ignore him," wrote columnist Neerja Chowdhury.

In 2012 Gujarat polls, Modi offered another new phenomenon in campaigning, the use of 3D and the novelty idea seemed to have excited voters more than the critics. In 2007, the Modi masks had similar effect. And who can dispute the impact of Aam Aadmi Party cap in Delhi elections in 2013?

In fact, as elections seemed to approach, Modi offers new idea at each interaction. On April 26, 2013, inaugurating Yoga Guru Baba Ramdev's Acharyakulam School in Haridwar in presence of influential spiritual leaders like Morari Bapu and Rameshji Oza; Modi said, "I am not just the leader of majority Hindus. I am the leader of Indians." In the words of president of the Centre for Policy Research, Pratap Bhanu Mehta, courtesy *The Indian Express*, "Modi represents a longing for centralisation in an age of dispersion, decisiveness in a milieu of indecision, growth amidst a fear of stagnation and Government in the face of raucous democracy."

MODITVA AMID AAM AADMI FACTOR

On December 8, 2013 when assembly election results poured in, BJP leaders could easily realize their past lapses. If two previous years 2011 and 2012 had gone down the memory lane for BJP as not living up to its potential and having left the 'opposition space' to Team Anna, the circa 2013 made the saffron party realize its folly especially in the context of emergence of Arvind Kejriwal-led Aam Aadmi Party.

The Delhi mandate although elevated BJP as the single largest party, an unprecedented faith reposed on the nascent outfit has made it squirm and possibly forced it to wonder whether AAP's 'unconventional' style of politics could checkmate BJP's desperate and determined bid to capture power in 2014.

A quick learner that BJP is, close on the heels of the Delhi's rather path-breaking verdict, the party strategists took a page out of AAP's style book and decided to resort to door-to-door campaigning. The strategy meet attended among others by its prime ministerial candidate Narendra Modi also decided to draw funds from the Gujarat chief minister's rallies—which of course have been drawing huge turnout. In its election manifesto, the party is also likely to incorporate 'state-specific issues'—another pointer from AAP.

On January 10, 2014, in another strategy meet the BJP central parliamentary board virtually decided to designate AAP as its chief rival replacing the Congress. "Today, Congress is not competition for us, they have lost all space. The BJP will strive to fill this space. Our mission is 272+ seats, we are working towards that," BJP general secretary Ananth Kumar said apparently indicating that the unconventional style of AAP is playing more on the party leaders' mind. Moreover, in its Hyderabad meet, the RSS leadership also had reportedly directed the BJP chief Rajnath Singh to fine tune the poll strategy and also give up any complacency in view of its victories in 2013 assembly polls.

For BJP realistic view is that the single biggest take away from 2013 assembly polls mandate has been that amid a season of saffron surge and latent approval for Narendra Modi as the next Prime Minister, the voters in the national capital threw up a revolutionary mandate showing for once that the anguish of the 'common man' has nearly touched its zenith. The sooner the realization it's better for the party. There is definitely an added urgency for the BJP strategy team to fine tune the working style and roadmap especially in the wake of unprecedented success of the newly launched Aam Aadmi Party in Delhi polls.

In retrospect, poll pundits and political rivals including the BJP had under-estimated AAP to the core that former BJP president Nitin Gadkari, along with Delhi unit BJP chief Vijay Goel, even had the audacity of describing Kejriwal's party a 'chillar party'. Another BJP leader Piyush Goyal had called it a 'vote cutter'.

Nevertheless, the mandate Delhi left a few odd lessons for BJP also which came so near the target. The BJP watchers say 15-years negligence of organisation and then in 2012 leaving it to ambitious Vijay Goel's whims and fancies played maximum spoilsport. There were other factors too, like the belated projection of Harsh Vardhan. This was almost replicating 1998 story when Sushma Swaraj was brought in similarly at the last moment and given only 15 days to save a government which was hit by onion crisis.

In the post-poll analysis, a number of BJP leaders went vocal. The likes of Dr. Murli Manohar Joshi and Arun Jaitley told a closed door party meeting that the delay in projecting Dr. Harsh Vardhan was one major factor. There were some more specific and candid talks too. A section of leaders maintained that BJP leadership leaving the opposition space to Team Anna in 2011 has in the ultimate analysis proved 'costliest mistake' especially in the context of Delhi results.

"In 2011 we left the entire Opposition space to Team Anna and players like Baba Ramdev. While Congress played its part by mismanaging the anti-corruption crusaders that led to the 'Aam Aadmi' phenomenon; BJP also failed," said a key party leader.

"The Congress-led UPA and the socio-political issues had given us enough opportunities to exploit. Had we played all the cards well, BJP should have been in a much stronger position today," the party leader said. Nitin Gadkari, who was made special in-charge, was also being attacked for his indecision and failure to rein in Vijay Goel.

At a later stage, senior leader Arun Jaitley, however, has analyzed things better. "The results of the assembly elections on 8th December 2013 indicated that Modi versus Rahul debate was being overstated. Both Modi and the BJP had a decisive edge. The Delhi election witnessed the emergence of Aam Aadmi Party as a new challenger. In the last one month, the Aam Aadmi Party has occupied a large part of media and mind space. It is a party born out of a reaction. Political hopefuls who have in the past contested elections without a party platform have queued up to join the new party. Some of the recruits have traditionally received more air-time than actual votes. Today, they have found a platform for their aspirations," he wrote in a blog piece on his website on 10 January 2014.

At the same time, he talks about the need for BJP and its PM-nominee Modi to chart out big agenda for the country. This is vital as it will make a clear distinction between AAP and BJP. Even otherwise, many voters in Delhi say while they voted for AAP in Delhi assembly polls, about four months ago (September-October 2013) they had decided to vote for 'Namo' for the Lok Sabha polls. Thus, BJP should be cautious about AAP but need not be scary. In terms of challenge they are far ahead of AAP and Modi definitely a better and time-tested leader as compared to inexperienced Arvind Kejriwal.

Kejriwal's game plan on curbing corruption is smart enough. Jaitley rightly pointed out: "The AAP is trying to alter the corruption agenda. There is no reference to corruption allegations which can embarrass the Congress. The CWG scam, the 2G spectrum allocation, Coal block allocation or corruption of the Sheila Dixit Government are not mentioned by it. It is deflecting the attention to petty corruption." He again pointed out the absence of any long term vision in AAP programme. "The AAP's Delhi Government's performance post the results has not been too inspiring. It has no agenda to evolve Delhi into a global city. Its Delhi activities have centred around the vehicles in which the Ministers travel, kind of houses they occupy, the freebies that they can distribute, how to sting people and other similar activities intended to occupy media centre stage. Some of these symbolisms may be important but they do not improve the quality of life of the ordinary citizen. These gimmicks do not have a lasting impact."

However, just as Jaitley says, no one can deny that "at least transiently there is a space" in several parts of the country for the new outfit, Aam Aadmi Party.

BJP and Modi's poll strategists need to address that issue in certain details. In Kolkata for instance, amid growing middle class frustration with Mamata regime after 35-year long rule of the Left, among Marwari and non-Bengali sections of people, there is a clamour for Aam Aadmi Party. In January 2014, as we visited Odisha, we found that even in temple city of Puri, commoners were talking about Kejriwal's outfit. There has been similar curiosity factor attached for a large section of people in cities like Bangalore.

But having said these, one also needs to caution that those who are seeking an association with AAP directly or indirectly are being actually self-seekers too.

On 10 January 2014, the day AAP announced enrolment of 1 crore foot-soldiers by 26th January, a Facebook posting candidly said: BEELINE FOR AAP: for many, the party is a short-cut to their political ambition ... it was also responded almost tongue-in-cheek fashion by another: A short-cut also means short circuit!!

This is precisely the big difference that BJP needs to project between itself and AAP—which is actually in the words of union minister Jairam Ramesh a 'conglomeration' of protest movement and in the words of BJP's Arun Jaitley, a party 'born out of reaction'.

Narendra Modi – A Profile

Narendra Damodardas Modi was born on 17 September 1950 in a family of grocers in Vadnagar in Mehsana district of what was then Bombay State (present-day Gujarat), India. He was the third of six children born to Damodardas Mulchand Modi and his wife, Heeraben. Modi ran a tea stall with his brother around a bus terminus. He completed his schooling in Vadnagar, where a teacher described him as being an average student but a keen debater.

He began work in the staff canteen of Gujarat State Road Transport Corporation, where he stayed till he became a full-time *Pracharak* (campaigner) of the RSS. After Modi had received RSS training in Nagpur, which was a prerequisite for taking up an official position in the Sangh Parivar, he was given charge of Sangh's student wing Akhil Bharatiya Vidyarthi Parishad (ABVP) in Gujarat. Modi organised agitations and covert distribution of Sangh's pamphlets during the Emergency. During his years in the RSS, Modi came in touch with Vasant Gajendragadkar and Nathalal Jaghda, leaders of the Jan Sangh, who later founded the BJP's

Gujarat state unit. Modi remained a *Pracharak* in the RSS while he completed his Master's degree in political science from Gujarat University.

The RSS seconded Modi to the BJP in 1987. While Shankarsinh Vaghela and Keshubhai Patel were the established names in the Gujarat BJP at that time, Modi rose to prominence after organising Murli Manohar Joshi's *Ekta Yatra* (journey for unity). His electoral strategy was central to BJP's victory in the 1995 state elections.

Modi became the General Secretary of the BJP and was transferred to New Delhi where he was assigned responsibility for the party's activities in Haryana and Himachal Pradesh. Vaghela, who had threatened to break away from BJP in 1995, defected from the BJP after he lost the 1996 Lok Sabha elections. In 1998, Modi was promoted to the post of National Secretary of the BJP. While selecting candidates for the 1998 state elections in Gujarat, Modi sidelined people who were loyal to Vaghela and rewarded those who favoured Patel, thus ending factional divisions within the party. His strategies were key to winning those elections.

Patel's failing health, allegations of abuse of power, corruption and poor administration, as well as loss of BJP seats in by-elections, prompted BJP's national leadership to seek a new candidate for the office of chief minister. Patel's position was also damaged by the devastating Bhuj Earthquake of 2001, the effects of which his administration struggled to handle. Modi, who had aired his misgivings about Patel's administration, was chosen as a replacement. L.K. Advani, a senior leader of the BJP, however, did not want to ostracise Patel and was worried about Modi's lack of experience in governance. It was suggested that Modi should be made the deputy chief minister in a government led by Patel, upon which Modi informed Advani and Atal Bihari Vajpayee that he was "going to be fully responsible for Gujarat or not at all" and declined the proposal. On 7 October 2001, Modi was appointed the Chief Minister of Gujarat and was assigned the responsibility to prepare the BJP for elections in December 2002. As Chief Minister, Modi's ideas of governance revolved around privatisation and small government.

On 27 February 2002, a train with several hundred passengers including large numbers of Hindu pilgrims was burned near Godhra, killing 58 people. Following rumours that the arson had been carried out by a Muslim mob, there was widespread anti-Muslim violence throughout Gujarat. The Gujarat administration was accused by human rights organizations, the opposition, and sections of the media of taking insufficient action against the violence, and condoning it in some cases. The Modi government imposed curfew in major cities, issued shoot-at-sight orders, and called for the army to prevent the violence from escalating. In April 2009, the Supreme Court of India appointed Special Investigation Team (SIT) to inquire into the Gujarat government and Narendra Modi's role in the incidents of communal violence. The SIT reported to the court in December 2010 submitting that they did not find any incriminating evidence against Modi of wilfully allowing communal violence in the state. Modi's decision to move the corpses of the *kar sevaks* who had been burned to death in Godhra to Ahmedabad has also been criticized for inflaming the violence. However, the SIT found his decision to be justified.

In April 2012, the SIT absolved Modi of any involvement in the Gulbarg Society massacre, one of the many riots that occurred in 2002. On 7 May 2012, the Supreme Court-appointed *amicus curiae*, Raju Ramachandran, observed that Modi could be prosecuted for promoting enmity among different groups during the 2002 Gujarat violence. His main contention was that the evidence should be examined by a court of law because the SIT was required to investigate but not to judge. The *amicus* report has been criticised by the Special Investigation Team for relying heavily on the testimony of Sanjiv Bhatt. In July 2013, it was alleged that SIT was suppressing evidence.

In the aftermath of the violence, there were calls for Modi to resign from his position as Chief Minister of Gujarat. Opposition parties stalled the Parliament. Both the Dravida Munnetra Kazhagam (DMK) and the Telugu Desam Party (TDP), allies of the BJP, also asked for Modi's resignation, as did Jayalalithaa, the then Chief Minister of Tamil Nadu and leader of the All India Anna Dravida Munnetra Kazhagam (AIADMK). Modi submitted his resignation and the state Assembly was dissolved. In the subsequent elections the BJP, led by Modi, won 127 seats in the 182-member assembly.

During his second term, Modi's emphasis shifted from Hindutva to the economic development of Gujarat. Modi's decisions curtailed the influence of organizations of Sangh Parivar such as the Bharatiya Kisan Sangh (BKS) and the Vishva Hindu Parishad (VHP), which had become entrenched in Gujarat after the decline of Ahmedabad's textile industry. Modi dropped Gordhan Zadaphia, an ally of his former Sangh co-worker and VHP state chief Praveen Togadia, from the ministry. Various organisations of the Sangh were no longer consulted or apprised of Modi's administrative decisions prior to enactment.

The changes brought by Modi in the period 2002-2007 has led to Gujarat being called an attractive investment destination. *Business Standard* writes that "there was sufficient anecdotal evidence pointing to the fact that corruption had gone down significantly in the state ... if there was to be any corruption, Modi had to know about it." Modi instituted financial and technology parks in the state. During the 2007 Vibrant Gujarat Summit, real estate investment deals worth

Rs. 6.6 trillion were signed in Gujarat.

Atal Bihari Vajpayee, the then Prime Minister of India, who had asked Modi not to discriminate between citizens in the aftermath of the 2002 Gujarat violence and had pushed for his resignation as Chief Minister of Gujarat, distanced himself from Modi and reached out to North Indian Muslims before 2004 Lok Sabha elections. After the elections, Vajpayee held the violence in Gujarat as one of the reasons for BJP's electoral defeat and acknowledged that not removing Modi immediately after the Gujarat violence was a mistake.

In the lead up to assembly and general elections in 2007-2008, the BJP stepped up its rhetoric on terrorism. On 18 July 2006, Modi criticised Prime Minister Manmohan Singh for his reluctance to revive anti-terror legislations such as the Prevention of Terrorist Activities Act. He asked the national government to allow states to invoke tougher laws in the wake of the 2006 blasts in Mumbai.

Around this time Modi frequently demanded the execution of Afzal Guru, a collaborator of Pakistani *jihadis*, who had been convicted of terrorism for his involvement in the 2001 Indian Parliament attack.

BJP won the 2007 election, gaining 122 of the 182 seats in the state assembly, and Modi continued in office as Chief Minister.

As a consequence of November 2008 Mumbai attacks, Modi held a meeting to discuss security of Gujarat's 1,600 km long coastline which resulted in the Central Government authorising making of 30 high-speed surveillance boats.

In recent years Gujarat has improved its agricultural output substantially, in large part due to projects relating to improvement of groundwater supply in Saurashtra, Kachchh and the north, as well as efforts to increase the use of micro-irrigation and to provide more efficient power supply to farms. Public irrigation measures in the central and southern areas, such as the Sardar Sarovar Project, have not been so successful in achieving their aims.

BJP governments under Patel and Modi supported NGOs and communities in the creation of infrastructure projects for conservation of groundwater. By December 2008, 5,00,000 structures had been constructed, of which 1,13,738 were check-dams. While most check-dams remained empty during the pre-monsoon season, they helped recharge the aquifers that lie beneath them. 60 of the 112 tehsils which were found to have over-exploited the groundwater table in 2004 had regained their normal groundwater level by 2010 and Gujarat managed to increase its groundwater levels at a time when they were falling in all other Indian states. As a result, production of genetically-modified Bt cotton, which could now be irrigated using tubewells, increased to become the largest in India. The boom in cotton production and utilization of semi-arid land saw the agricultural growth rate of Gujarat increase to 9.6 per cent in the period 2001-2007. For the decade 2001-2010, Gujarat recorded a compound annual growth rate of 10.97 per cent, the highest among all Indian states.

The system of supplying power to rural areas has been changed radically and has had a greater impact on agriculture than the irrigation works. With the Jyotigram Yojana, based on ideas developed by the International Water Management Institute, agricultural supplies were rewired to separate them from other rural supplies and then the electricity used by farmers was rationed to fit with scheduled demand for irrigation and consequently to reduce the amount of subsidy being paid.

Modi's government worked to brand Gujarat as a state of dynamic development and economic growth and prosperity, using the slogan 'Vibrant Gujarat'. Officials from the state of Gujarat claim that Gujarat outperformed India as a whole in the rates of improvement of multiple human indicators such as female education, between 2001 and 2011. Furthermore, they state that dropout rates declined from 20 per cent in 2001 to 2 per cent in 2011, and maternal mortality declined by 32 per cent from 2001 to 2011.

During late 2011 and early 2012, Modi undertook a series of fasts as part of *Sadbhavna* Fast, meant to reach out to the Muslim community in Gujarat. Modi announced that he believed that his fast would "further strengthen Gujarat's environment of peace, unity and harmony."

Sadbhavna Fast (17-19 September 2011) started in Ahmedabad aimed at strengthening the atmosphere of peace, unity, and harmony in the state. He observed 36 fasts in 26 districts and 8 cities.

In the 2012 Gujarat legislative assembly elections, Modi won from the constituency of Maninagar with a majority of 86,373 votes over Sanjiv Bhatt's wife Shweta, who was contesting for the Indian National Congress. The BJP as a whole won 115 of the 182 seats; it has formed the government in Gujarat since 1995 and has had an absolute majority throughout Modi's time in office.

Later in the by-elections for 6 seats, the BJP won all the seats in Gujarat which consisted of four assembly seats and 2 Lok Sabha seats. Interestingly, BJP won all these seats although Modi never campaigned for its candidates and all the seats were held by the Congress prior to the by-elections. This brought up the number of seats held by the BJP in the state assembly to 119.

To attract foreign investment in Gujarat during his time as Chief Minister, Modi has made visits to countries such as China, Singapore and Japan.

Modi is a vegetarian. He is known for leading a frugal lifestyle and has a personal staff of three. He is known to be a workaholic and an introvert. He is a crowd-puller as a speaker.

British economist Jim O'Neill, author of the BRIC report, wrote on his blog that Modi is 'good on economics', one of the things that 'India desperately needs in a leader'. In August 2013, financial analyst Chris Wood, chief strategist of CLSA, wrote in his weekly *Greed and Fear* that "the Indian stock market's greatest hope is the emergence of Gujarat Chief Minister Narendra Modi as the BJP's Prime Ministerial candidate."

In March 2013, Modi was appointed as member of the BJP Parliamentary Board, its highest decision-making body, and also as Chairman of the party's Central Election Campaign Committee. Modi was selected to head the poll campaign for 2014 parliamentary election, at the national level executive meeting of BJP on 10 June 2012.

In September 2013, BJP announced Modi as Prime Ministerial candidate for the 2014 Lok Sabha polls.

Modi promised to develop 100 smart cities, set-up IITs, IIMs and AIIMS in every state, and bullet trains to all four corners of the country. Modi highlighted his way of development in all walks of life—education, social upliftment, law and order, employment, agriculture, foreign relations, defence, etc. etc.

On his plans to build "brand India" to compete in the globalised world, he said his government, if formed, would focus on 5-Ts—talent, tradition, tourism, trade and technology.

Other priorities in Modi's programme include development of infrastructure such as roads, ports and airports, reviving power plants that are shut, creating jobs, skill development, setting up agro infrastructure gas grids, deploying optical fibre networks, pushing the river interlinking project and establishing special courts to punish black marketing.

Appendix

Interview of Jashodaben

The man she claims is still her 'husband' is the BJP's Prime Ministerial candidate Narendra Modi, Chief Minister of Gujarat. Jashodaben, 62, a retired school teacher who gets a monthly pension of Rs. 14,000, lives mostly with a brother and spends much of her time in prayer. In Ahmedabad to visit her extended family, she agreed to be interviewed by *The Indian Express* but refused to be photographed. Excerpts from her first interview since Modi was named PM candidate:

Q. *For how long were you married and what is the status of the marriage?*

A. We married when I was 17... I had quit studies once I went to his place and remember him saying he wanted me to pursue my education. He would mostly talk to me about completing my education. Initially he took interest in talking to me and even in the affairs of the kitchen.

Q. *Do you feel burdened by the relationship, especially when the media asks you about your strained relationship? Are you instructed to remain low profile?*

A. We have never been in touch and we parted on good terms as there were never any fights between us. I will not make up things that are not true. In three years, we may have been together for all of three months. There has been no communication from his end to this day.

Q. *Do you track the news about Narendra Modi?*

A. Yes, I read everything that I can get my hands on. I read all the newspaper articles and also watch news on the television and like to read about him.

Q. *If he becomes the next Prime Minister and moves to Delhi, would you like to go back to him, if he calls you back? Will you try and meet him?*

A. I have never gone to meet him and we have never been in touch. I don't think he will ever call me. In whatever I say, I do not want it to harm him. I just wish that he progresses in whatever he does. I know he will become PM one day!

Q. *Did he ever tell you he was leaving you or quitting the marriage?*

A. He told me once that "I will be travelling across the country and will go as and where I please; what will you do following me?" When I came to Vadnagar to live with his family, he told me "why did you come to your in-laws' house when you are still so young, you must instead focus on pursuing your studies". The decision to leave was my own and there was never any conflict between us. He never spoke to me about the RSS or about his political leanings. When he told me he would be moving around the country as he wished, I told him I would like to join him. However, on many occasions when I went to my in-laws' place, he would not be present and he stopped coming there. He used to spend a lot of time in RSS shakhas. So I too stopped going there after a point and I went back to my father's house.

Q. *Are you still legally Modi's wife?*

A. Every time people take his name, I am also mentioned somewhere, even though in the background. Did you not come all the way and look all over, to find me and come and speak to me? If I was not his wife, would you have come to speak to me?

Q. *Do you feel slighted that your status as a wife has not been acknowledged by him in all these years?*

A. No. I don't feel bad, because I know that he is doing so due to destiny and bad times. In such situations he has to say such things and also has to lie. I don't see my situation as being bad because I feel, in a way, my luck has improved too.

Q. *Why have you never remarried?*

A. After this experience, I don't think I want to. My heart is not into it.

Q. *How did you support yourself after you moved back to your parents' house?*

A. My in-laws treated me well, but would never speak about the marriage. My father paid the fees for my studies and I also got some financial assistance from my brothers to continue my education. I had lost my mother when I was two years old and I lost my father two years after I started studying again and was in class 10. However,

Gandhi dynasty that dominated Indian politics for the past decade suffered a crushing blow. Out of 543, Congress secured just 44 seats, its worst-ever tally.

Mayawati's Bahujan Samaj Party (BSP) wiped out in the elections. Samajwadi Party (SP) got only 6 seats in UP.

Aam Aadmi Party's (AAP) chief, Arvind Kejriwal, fell well short of Modi in Varanasi. His party badly collapsed due to its breach of trust in Delhi and immature acts.

US President Barack Obama called Narendra Modi to congratulate him on the Bharatiya Janata Party's success in India's historic election offering a fresh start to a relationship bruised by a decision years ago not to let Modi into the US. The President noted he looks forward to work closely with Mr. Modi to fulfill the extraordinary promise of the US-India strategic partnership, and they agreed to continue expanding and deepening the wide-ranging cooperation between the two democracies. Obama invited Narendra Modi to visit Washington at a mutually agreeable time to further strengthen bilateral relationship.

Pakistan Prime Minister Nawaz Sharif offered his congratulations and good wishes on Bhartaya Janata Party's impressive victory in the elections in India. On his part, during campaign, Modi emphasised the need for India and Pakistan to fight against poverty. Many other foreign dignitaries also congratulated Narendra Modi for his victory.

Narendra Modi, was sworn in as Prime Minister (PM) by President Pranab Mukherjee ten years after the previous National Democratic Alliance (NDA) Government in 2004. Narendra Modi was sworn in along with his confidant Cabinet colleagues.

Now appx 1.25 million people of India are looking to team Modi for overall development and solutions of some major problems like inflation, national security, corruption, unemployment and other problems.

Index